T0284232

HEREAFTER

Hereafter

THE TELLING LIFE OF ELLEN O'HARA

Vona Groarke

NEW YORK UNIVERSITY PRESS
New York

NEW YORK UNIVERSITY PRESS
New York
www.nyupress.org

© 2022 by New York University
All rights reserved

Interior design by Frances Baca

References to Internet websites (URLs) were accurate at the time of writing.
Neither the author nor New York University Press is responsible for URLs that
may have expired or changed since the manuscript was prepared.

Please contact the Library of Congress for Cataloging-in-Publication data.

ISBN: 9781479817511 (hardback)
ISBN: 9781479817535 (library ebook)
ISBN: 9781479817528 (consumer ebook)

New York University Press books are printed on acid-free paper, and their binding
materials are chosen for strength and durability. We strive to use environmentally
responsible suppliers and materials to the greatest extent possible in publishing
our books.

Manufactured in the United States of America

10 9 8 7 6 5 4 3 2 1

Also available as an ebook

For
EVE ELLEN
next in line

and in memory of my mother
HELEN
whose stories were the source.

Contents

List of Figures

Note on the Poems

I have chosen to situate Ellen's voice within a form I think of as a "folk sonnet," less interested in meter than it is in the structure of the boxy fourteen-line rhyming form, however loosely deployed. I imagine that Ellen, a busy housekeeper all her life, would have cherished its neat containment and no-nonsense air.

Ellen's sonnets ask the form to breathe in the details of an "unheroic" life and to breathe out a rangy line, a tone of voice, and an attitude. She came to me first as a boxy, skeptical, self-assured, but traditional woman often keener on privacy than on frank outpouring. With its inbuilt pivot of silence, its *volta*, the Italian sonnet (made howsoever plastic here) seemed a natural fit.

Saint Attracta

Once upon a time there was a monster out at
Glenavoo who used to go around devouring
the cattle and crops of the place, all the
people were afraid of it untill Saint
Attracta came and chased him down a hill
and put him into a hole and blessed a
well that there. She then gave the water
to the people to sprinkle on their crops
and homes, and that no harm would come
to them. Glenavoo is a townland in
the parish of Kilmacteige in County Sligo
Stations are performed there every year
on the last Sunday of July.

Obtained from my   Brigid M McIntyre
     Father   Leitrim North
Pat McIntyre.   Cloonacool
     50.   Co, Sligo

Primary school student's description of Saint Attracta, 1938. National Folklore
Collection Schools 172:79; Pat McIntyre (50), Leitrim North, County Sligo. Collector:
Brigid McIntyre, Corsallagh National School, County Sligo, 1938. Teacher: Tomás
O'Ceallaigh.

Prologue

Glenavoo, Co. Sligo: where you came from. Come from.

That Glenavoo (*Gleann na bhFuath* in the Irish language) could mean either 'Glen of Ghosts' or 'Glen of Hatred' is not lost on me.

> **fuath**$_1$, *m*. 1. *Lit*: Form, shape.
> 2. Phantom, spectre.
> **fuath**$_2$, *m*. Hate, hatred.
> (*TEANGLANN.IE*)

Saint Attracta: Patron Saint of Glenavoo

> *Sixth-century daughter of an Irish noble. Miracle worker and noted healer . . . with powers against warts and rickets . . .*
>
> *Venerated in her own day and in the Middle Ages when many popular (i.e. fantastic) biographies of her circulated.*
> —*HTTPS://CATHOLICSAINTS.INFO*

Fantastic biographies, indeed.

ONE

Being Here

My great-grandmother stops by today to check in on me.
She makes tea from leaves and bids me drain it quickly,
for once in my life, not to speak. Looking into the cup,
she tells me to buy a bicycle, grow my hair and wear it up,
that a man I don't know thinks ardently of me, that number six
will be significant, and that I should have my eyes checked.

It seems she gets by by fortune-telling on the other side:
no version of the future, she says, is wasted on the dead.

It's true my eyes have been feeling the strain of hour on hour
screen-gleaning for verifiable facts. I started with no more
than her name; now I have a list of questions to put to her
that she doesn't seem, to be frank, inclined to answer.
She tilts the leaves, examining, but gives no more commands,
then gones herself into thin air. The small, white cup remains.

What am I to do with her now, how should I have her dress?
Fur-collared greatcoat; green-ribboned hat; stout, invincible shoes?
I need her to look great-grandmotherly, if I'm to believe in her
but having known only one grandparent, scantly (her daughter),
I'm not sure how to begin. With a headstone handbag at her feet
with her whole life inside? She doesn't so much as glance at it.
The look I give her giving me dares me give her paste earrings,
a tortoiseshell clip in her hair. I give her, instead, a herring

-bone tweed skirt, little spectacles, the necessary gold band,
a walking stick (Where did this come from?) in her hand,
and a brooch of a harp pinned to her coat, lest anyone
not know by looking at her face where she comes from.
I dress her in a life that seems to me plausible, if not true.
"You have beautiful hands," I say. She doesn't answer me.

I CONJURE YOU out of the single fact that once you lived, and the living was done, for the most part, here. In this city, New York, where I am living for the term of a fellowship at the Cullman Center in the New York Public Library (NYPL).

I didn't come to write about you, but, somewhere along the line, out of casual curiosity, I start in on you, Ellen O'Hara, and, once I do, I'm hooked.

My mother knew you when she was a child, before she left to live in Ireland. You were in her stories, and the way she told them left me in no doubt that she loved you best of all. I have no concrete evidence: no photograph, diary, letter, document—no object I know for sure passed through your hands.

There was a life, the fact of it, the secondhand memories of it. And that's what I have to work with.

A lot slips through a life: clothes, money, habits, health, friends, family, homes, and countries. The songs you hummed. The hats you chose. Your accent and voice. Your handwriting. The shape of the body you lived in. What made you laugh.

Your life was porous as a piece of muslin, stretched between the side-seams of the facts of birth and death.

At NYPL, so much of the knowledge of the world is mine to call up, to have (literally) brought to my door. I can ask questions, and if they're practical questions, the answer will ring clear and true.

But a life is more than practical questions with their fixed and adequate answers. A life is a miasma of what can be explained and understood, and what really can't.

My job in this, it seems clear to me, is to find a way to answer for what is known and what is not. To do so I will need guard-rail prose, but I will also need language that cross-stitches and embroiders itself, the way poetry often does.

There will be fact and doubt and speculation; there will be imagining.

And there will be a story that skeins between two chairs that face each other in this room, for you and I to occupy.

I am going to tell your life and you are going to help me, Ellen O'Hara, of whom I am a sort of thin-veined proof.

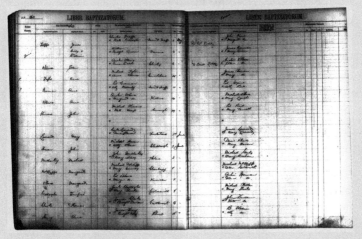

Baptism register for the parish of Kilmacteigue (1845–1880). Ellen O'Hara is the second entry from the top. Image courtesy of the National Library of Ireland, Microfilm 04226/08, 88.

I START WITH A NAME AND A PLACE: Ellen O'Hara from Aclare in County Sligo.

The only thing I can be certain of is that, in the third quarter of the nineteenth century in rural Sligo, there's no way you were not baptized.

Two hours and thirteen minutes of searching through the handwritten baptism register for Kilmacteigue (1845–80), and there you are: Ellen O'Hara, daughter of Austin O'Hara and Anne Walsh; baptized on May 6, 1862; place of residence, Glenavoo (a townland close to the village of Aclare), which is sometimes written as Glenawoo, one consonant halving and doubling itself as though it were the moon.

Eleven other children were born after you, the last being Sarah (Sally), born in 1885, by which time you'll have been gone for three years.

There you are, twelve siblings, your heads popping up in various places: parish registers for baptisms and marriages, passenger and immigration records, the U.S. census, and the Irish one.

If you'd wanted to hide, you've have found it difficult. But why would you hide from me?

WHY TAKE IT ON, THIS STORY? Why set myself on a trail of scattered research crumbs, no end in sight, maybe no end possible that could account for all these words?

You see an orange on a gate pillar in the countryside, you can't help yourself, you're wrapping it in narrative to take away with you. Who gave it to her, why he did, why she didn't eat it, and why she decided to leave it just here.

Story is company.

And so we look for shapes in clouds, so we can hear ourselves give them a name.

And so we see bearded faces peer back at us from the heart of the fire.

And we say the pattern in the carpet looks uncannily like the profile of someone we used to love, one time.

From there, it is only a very little crossing to the thought that nothing is ever really lost.

Because if birds sing the syllables of a name. And a shadow falls where no shadow should be. And words still mean what they did when we wrote them, we cannot be alone.

Nor am I.

I have whole lives in mine.

TWO
The Long Shadow

I AM TRYING TO LOOK BEHIND YOU, to what was at your back; to what molded and decided you, and trimmed.

As if you were some sort of ghost, to be seen clean through.

I hadn't thought of this as a famine story, but of course it is.

Austin was born in 1831, Anne in 1835: they were of an age by the time of the Great Famine (1845–52) to experience it firsthand and irrevocably.

Who knows what the nature of that experience might have been, how it might have inflected their house and twelve children, growing up in the shadow of that catastrophe?

"Twenty-five years later, when we were young, we'd still hear
terrible stories you'd try to unhear after, but you never could,
stories you'd think couldn't possibly be true, except they were.
A baby crying all night, the neighbors afraid to go in a house
where the fever had stricken everyone in the family, almost.
Cries thinning out until, at last, they stopped: a silence so loud,
it drove the next-door woman mad. They say she killed
her baby and then suckled him, not seeing he was dead.

"First, animals were sold, then hens, furniture, blankets, shoes.
Last to go was the clothes they stood up in, but they went too.
They died in rags, barefoot. And they died in ditches. In rain
and sleet and snow. Eating grass and nettles, sucking stones.
Nothing between a freezing wind and their loose bones but skin;
nothing between their living and dying but that freezing wind."

"Destitution in Ireland—Failure of the Potato Crop," *Pictorial Times*, August 22, 1846. Image courtesy of the National Library of Ireland, PD2120 TX (2) 49.

This parish [Kilmacteigue] comprising a very extensive tract of mountainous district was at all times remarkable for the poverty and destitution of its inhabitants. It has suffered more from the potato blight than any other locality in this country. . . . In many districts the old and young are literally naked, having neither shoes nor clothes.

—LETTER FROM REV. ROGER BRENNAN ADM TO SOCIETY OF FRIENDS' CLOTHING DEPARTMENT, DECEMBER 29, 1847, QUOTED IN SWORDS (1999, 265)

The district [Upper Leyny] contains a population of about 27,000 inhabitants of whom about 20,000 are in a state of destitution.

—LETTER FROM DEAN HOARE TO WILLIAM STANLEY, MARCH 10, 1847, QUOTED IN SWORDS (1999, 155)

A wide swathe of counties lost more than 20% of their populations and a few . . . (including Sligo). . . lost close to 30%.

—LIAM KENNEDY, PAUL ELL, E. M. CRAWFORD, AND L. A. CLARKSON (1999, 26)

"It wasn't hunger that drove me here, though that wasn't so for some.
 Our smallholding was more or less sufficient when good harvest came
 and enough of us to make good headway with hard work on the land.
 But every home is different, and not always blessed with willing hands
 or a fair wind. Three years before I left for here, there was a bad harvest,
 famine, fever like in Black '47, a foul smell, the Tubbercurry workhouse,
 built for five hundred, crammed with eight. More on the roadside,
 more still on the ships to America, out of sight of the graveyard.

"It was an autumn harvest of strange noises on the wind:
 a punch of heat or a veil of cold that could not be explained,
 a patch of shadow you'd walk on and feel chilled to the bone,
 cries and pleas for help from children where there were none.
 My father, who'd lived through it all before, and worse
 said he saw no life worth our living in a place so cursed."

"What else I heard pulled from the dark box of the famine years:
a man who pawned his cabin door for a shilling to buy meal.
Bailiffs seizing the blanket, throwing the baby to the floor,
taking the empty cooking pot from its hook above the fire,
pulling shawls off women's backs, shoes off the feet of men
(who'd not be taken then for public works, breaking stones
or building roads), all to be auctioned in the landlord's name
and him over in London, mostly, without charity or shame.

"To clear a paddock, the same landlord turned two families out
when they fell behind on rent. But the mare was a lovely sight
in the clean, new field. And finer still on the roasting spit
from which she fed the townland like her owner never did.
A lad was hanged. On the scaffold, he said they did him right
for he'd far rather hang quickly than starve bitterly to death."

"I can't give you much else: people hated to talk about it.
Mama and Dada would bless themselves and remain mute
as stones if we asked. You'd almost swear they were untrue,
the stories we learned listening to the wind wheedle names
from gaps in clumps of stones where houses used to be.
Or picking out lazy-beds poking through the skin of farms
where people lived and ate and tended crops that closed
over the past. But the land remembered, if people refused.

"Now and then a name, followed by 'God rest her soul,'
or a patch of road hurried past when there was no call.
The field with no cross said to be brimming with dead,
thin bones rattling when a rook alit, if you listened hard.
A shard of cup seen in a ditch where no cup ought to be.
Silence to fill a church if we asked, 'Did any of us die?'"

NOT EVERYONE IN THESE PARISHES WAS DESTITUTE. Some lived in fine houses with bed linen and beds in which they slept soundly, full-bellied, while others around them starved.

Not all of them were landlords. But some of them were.

From my reading, I conclude that if your landlord was in residence on his Irish estate, you stood some chance, at least, of clemency from him during the worst years.

In 1847, Major Brabazon of Tubbercurry, for example (who had already offered abatements in rent and advised his tenants not to sell their corn to pay him rent), opened two soup kitchens in Tubbercurry for the free distribution of food and shelter for the homeless, as the workhouse could no longer hold all the destitute.*

But if your landlord lived in England, as so many of them did, it seemed a very easy thing to instruct your agent to collect rent, as usual, from tenants who were a miasma of abstracted distress. No one you'd have to look in the eye as you took his money from him on a cross-quarter day. Or see him one day on the road carrying a coffin with his child in it.

Glenavoo had no resident landlord.

I try to imagine rent day, men standing in line to hand over money to the landlord's agent—hungry men, probably, in dire need of that money to buy meal for their families. How do you even put together the rent when everything you own has already been pawned, and you have no seed to plant next year's crop, and maybe not the health to plant it if you had?

How would you ever forget that? How would you steer clear of the bitterness and rage that must have framed your sense of the world and your place in it? How would you not pass that on to your children, and accept from them whatever help they could offer, at whatever the cost, to get out from under it?

....

* *An Gorta Mór*, 54.

Over one million people died and an even greater number emigrated during a six-year period, thus cutting the population by over 25 per cent.
—CHRISTINE KINEALY (2002, 2)

Nothing but the successive failures of the potato could have produced the emigration which will, I trust, give us room to become civilized.
—W. S. TRENCH, LORD LANSDOWNE'S AGENT (1852)
QUOTED IN TÓIBÍN AND FERRITER (2001, 24)

In 1845, there were 97,000 Irish men, women and children in New York City. By 1855, that number was almost doubled, and Irish-born New Yorkers comprised almost one-third of the city's total population.
—ANNELISE H. SHROUT (2012, 536)

"One other thing I remember is people not using the word 'soup';
  it was like it was a sullied, shameful word, an insult to offer you.
  Some still had the Irish, *anraith*, or said 'pottage.' We said 'broth':
  Dada said we should have English words in case we went abroad.
  Abroad. That was a little word that had a big world packed inside.
  We thought Galway was abroad, don't mind Boston or Adelaide.
  But of course we knew America on Mr. Ford's colored map
  and we knew getting there was to cross water on a big ship.

"I never thought it would be me crossing. I thought such a journey
  was bigger than me, that I'd never manage it or have reason to.
  I was all for staying home when I was young, tending the hens
  and the orphan lambs, helping with the babies and washing,
  making broth. I had as much notion of climbing on a ship
  to sail off to New York City as I did of dancing with a pig."

"Of course, I knew plenty other people who had gone,
 neighbors, older sisters, some of them kith and kin.
 Dada's cousin Eileen went in 1847, sent home a letter
 in someone else's hand about her 'situation' as a cutter
 in a Lowell mill. That was the last they heard of her.
 He said her brother placed a notice in a newspaper,
 but there was never a reply. She fairly disappeared.
 You could be lost in America as you couldn't in Aclare.

"Dada said we should be able to write our own letters.
 I think that was why he let us stay so long at school,
 book-learning, as he said, being little weight to haul.
 For most people leaving, it wasn't the pull of better
 but the push of worse. Worse was nothing but hunger.
 Worse was living in a ditch. Worse still was dying there."

I AM THE DESCENDANT OF PEOPLE WHO SURVIVED, somehow, the famines in Glenavoo.

Of course I am.

But if they survived, they cannot have forgotten.

Austin and Anne must have known or seen people who starved or died of fever. Perhaps they'd gone hungry themselves, or been ill. Even if their families had been very, very lucky, they can't have been lucky enough to survive unscathed.

Did they talk about it, I wonder, with their children? Every harvest, did they smell the wind for a telltale stench? Were their hearts in their mouths when the spade went in, for fear of what would be lifted, for fear of the horror again?

And when the next (albeit less ferocious) famine did come down on them in 1879; when word came of divine apparitions over at Knock, not twenty miles away; when they heard, maybe, of a neighbor's son or daughter buying passage on a ship, did Austin and Anne look at their children and wonder about a world elsewhere, and, one day, hatch a plan?

THREE
Going and Coming

I can't be sure, exactly, why you left, but it's not that difficult to come up with possible reasons.

The family home, according to the 1900 census, was a third-class, two-roomed dwelling with a thatched roof and two windows to the front. By the time you left, the family numbered thirteen in all: that's a lot of people to be squeezed into those scant rooms.

There was precious little work off the farm for a young woman such as Ellen; if she wanted cash and independence, she was unlikely to pin down either by staying home. And if it was marriage she craved, and children, she may have looked at a dwindling male population and decided to try a future elsewhere, as so many around her were doing.

Between 1880 and 1890, 808,116 people left Ireland, 708,612 of them immigrating to the United States.*

Ellen is one.

....

* Schrier (1957, 157).

In the late 1870s and the 1880s poor harvests, evictions, agrarian turmoil and, most important, steep price declines for Irish farm products combined with renewed economic growth in the United States to produce a new wave of departures.
—KERBY MILLER (1985, 347)

In 1881 nearly 50 percent of Irish-born people were not living in Ireland.
—TIMOTHY GUINNANE (1997, 104)

Their primary reasons for emigration were economic: except for a favored few who could aspire to become national schoolteachers, the only employment opportunities for rural women were in domestic service; but that was regarded as so low in status that no parent or girl would consider it except under dire necessity. However, no disparagement attached to any kind of employment in America.
—KERBY MILLER (1985, 407)

Irish emigrants after the famine consisted overwhelmingly of single, young adults. . . . No other country's emigrants included so many women.
—TIMOTHY GUINNANE (1997, 105)

Searching passenger lists using her year of birth yields just three Ellen O'Haras. I feel like I'm closing in.

1. Arrived on the *City of Montreal*, 27/3/1882, Ellen O'Hara, aged 19, Spinster. (Right name, right age.)

2. Arrived on the *City of Chester*, 26/2/1883, Ellen O'Hara (later transcribed as Ellen Ottario), aged 20, Female, Servant. Her berth is "After Steerage," along with nine other females on this page. (Right name, right age.)

3. Arrived on the *City of Berlin*, 17/7/1882, Ellen O'Hara, aged 20, Spinster. (Right name, right age.)

The entry under hers reads "Kath O'Hara, aged 18, Spinster." A cousin? It makes sense: Ellen as the older girl, already big sister to nine siblings, used to managing.

This Ellen could be my Ellen. Any of these three could.

It's a question of picking one, of allowing the few bald details recorded on the passenger lists to seem to add up to a narrative, which is about as much as any realist could ask of a few facts.

Sligo—New York, July 1882

I'm guessing you board the Midland Great Western Railway
Ballina to Dublin train at Foxford, the nearest station to Glenavoo.

Someone will have gone with you, I'm sure, to Foxford, fourteen miles away, to help with your bag (not that it's so heavy).
There's the black coat your mother saved up egg money for. Your
only boots are on your feet. A nightdress Maggie made, with a
flower stitched in yellow on each cuff. And two day dresses you
cut out yourself, both from the same length of cotton so as not to
waste money on scraps.

Your mother has given you rosary beads. Your father gives
you a pen.

I'm not even going to try to imagine the saying goodbye.

Change in Athlone for the Limerick train. Change at Limerick for
Cork. Change at Cork for Queenstown, where the transatlantic
steamers from Liverpool and Southampton called, en route to
America.

"The SS *City of Berlin* Outward Bound Passing Cape Pine Lighthouse," by Samuel Walters (ca. 1876). Image courtesy of Wikimedia Commons.

"I'd never been further than Ballina, and only in the back of a cart.
The train shuffled field after tree after field, as Dada did with cards
and me as a spindle at the heart of it, the last still thing in the world.
It was as well, maybe, the departure was giddy so I thought the whirl
meant more than the leaving. For a while. Queenstown was a hell
of shouting and shoving and crying in the lurk of those huge hulls.
Beggars, drunks; porters who'd offer to carry bags, then disappear.
A mad woman pulling at me, asking was I not Bríd from Inis Oirr.

"That packed cabin was the most at home I'd felt since Glenavoo:
warm bodies close around me, women snoring as Mama used do,
a baby crying and someone being sick and someone whispering.
But only one privy for every hundred bunks on the *City of Berlin*
and no deck below in third class: for six nights, the same foul air.
Getting on, I knew nothing of Berlin. Getting off, I didn't care."

Laws made by men shut [girls] out of all hope of inheritance in their native land; their male relatives exploited their labour and returned them never a penny as reward, and finally, when at last their labour could not wring sufficient from the meagre soil to satisfy the exertions of all, these girls were incontinently packed across the ocean.

—JAMES CONNOLLY ([1915] 1968, 47)

It is the old people who remain in Ireland; those who must unavoidably be a burden on the community. It is the young and strong who go; the young men and women who would be a profit instead of a loss to the county, the flower and hope of the nation. Emigration takes the best.

—LOUIS PAUL-DUBOIS (1908, 355)

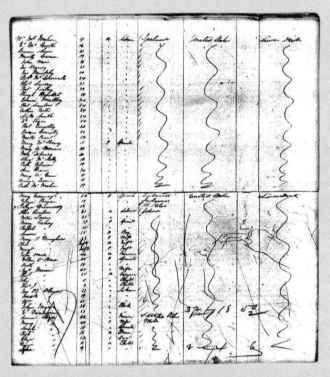

Passenger manifest from the SS *City of Berlin*, arrived in New York, July 17, 1882. Ellen O'Hara is listed eighteen lines from the bottom. Original data: passenger lists of vessels arriving in New York City, 1820–1897. Microfilm publication M237, 675 rolls. NAI: 6256867. Records of the U.S. Customs Service, Record Group 36. National Archives at Washington, DC.

"The first night when I settled myself down on that stiff bunk
I turned my back on the ocean and wished I was solid rock
instead of being like Carrageen moss, tide-tossed up and down.
But you can't turn away from water in a ship. It prowls around
like a famished cur no dream of home could soothe. Not even
hungry dogs, however, would eat the food we were given.

"Many the thing I saw new to me: teeth that came out at night,
a blind boy who'd wink at girls, a dead baby, twins, and a man
who'd draw your likeness if you'd kiss him later by the stairs,
which I did not. Someone had a squeeze-box. A girl with hair
down past her waist gave us 'The Harp That Once.' And after it
was silence but for waves on the hull like a fist on a bodhrán.

"New words I had no meaning for: *embark*, *knots*, *electric*, *stairs*,
all in a mess of accents, so you didn't know where you were."

THE LAST DAY, I IMAGINE, even the third-class passengers were allowed up on deck to see the city they would shortly enter as pilgrims, adventurers, survivors: immigrants.

The Statue of Liberty had not yet been erected, so the view would have been of stubs of buildings, all huddled in, and an occasional steeple or spire. Not the skyscrapers of today, of course, but if they were only three or four storeys, still taller than you would have seen before, even in Sligo town.

It's July 17: New York will have been pulling itself up to the height of its summer heat. That must have meant a sheen on the city that scattered as they neared. Like it was Hy-Brasil, the mythical island off the west of Ireland, cloaked in its phantom mist.

Whatever clothes you wore leaving Ireland will be smelly and stained and burdensome, I'd say, already thickening with heat.

But whatever discomfort you felt that day must have been at least in some way allayed by the sight of the shimmering, magical city becoming real before your eyes.

"ELLEN O'HARA." You give your name to the man with the moustache like slugs on his lips at the desk in Castle Garden. I put you down for sturdy and dark-haired, blue-eyed, like we are, mostly, in your line.

Brave-faced, I have you walk into the noisiest room you've ever been in, men shouting orders, your papers tight in your fist, your coat drawn tight around you despite the heat. You answer "Yes" to "Read and write?" "Maid" or "Servant," because that is what you've been taught to say. "Ireland." (How strange that word must be, never so used by you before as in the last two weeks.)

It's too lonely, all too much. I don't want you to be alone in this room, all these strangers, more people than you've ever seen in one place, and nobody you know.

So I grant you again that cousin, Kath, to stand behind you so she can hear your answers and lean into the words. You wait for her on the other side of the desk. When she walks to you, you turn to face the way she does, and the two of you, with your bags held tight, walk out through the door that's as high as three doors at home, out into a new world.

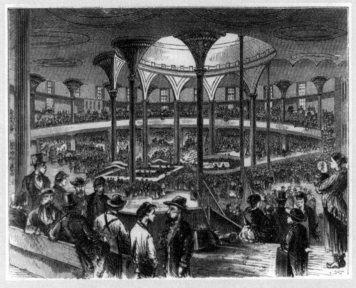

"Interior of Castle Garden" [no date recorded on caption card]. Image courtesy of the Library of Congress, Prints and Photographs Division, Washington, DC.

As they step out, so do I, into the straight path of a general story: a story not just of Ellen or Kath, but of young Irish immigrant women. They bring with them to this new world a basic education and domestic skills limited to the goings-on of a two-roomed cottage and fifteen acres, everything they own in a carpet bag they can easily lift and nothing in it as important as the name they keep close in to them of someone, an aunt or a neighbor's cousin, who they hope will unriddle this city for them and set them on their way.

With one character I allow myself to believe I'm listening, in receiver mode. But with two and a setting (the beginnings of plot), I can hear the machine of my own invention whirring. I am making it up, no doubt about it. And I find I enjoy them, these liberties I grant myself and these liberties I take.

Is it generous or dangerous, this wild imagining? For my part, I don't know.

I sit in a library office, surrounded by the facts of the world and not a few likewise imaginings. Which, I wonder, tells more truth?

In the offices beside mine are a biographer, a political scientist, a historian, and a novelist. I am poet-in-the-middle, tossing up facts into the air that fall again as conjecture, as confetti-like detail. Is this dishonest? Is it presumptuous? Does it dishonor your life and all your lives, having no way to gauge the full span of its inaccuracy?

But the facts are tombstones: dead-end truth. And the facts make so little room for a space we might call "Ellen" or "Kath," so briskly do they pass over the milling immigrants in that room.

The facts, despite all their minute and scrupulous attention, incline to the general. And the general interests me as backdrop only. Rightly or wrongly, I want to select one body from the throng, yours, and observing carefully, to draw first an outline, then to infill color and shade, and to make of them an intimating life.

"Haven't you a powerful imagination, all the same?" she says.
"You'd swear you were there." She has returned, unbidden,
 carrying an empty birdcage she doesn't bother to explain.
"Fiction, I tell you, fairy stories—most of it, downright lies."
 I think it's a story worth the telling, and what harm can it do?
"As if," she says, "this is a harm you might have any claim to.
 You'd do well to tend your own wounds but sure, I'll play along.
 If only to keep you halfway right. Or at least not fully wrong."

She puts the birdcage up on top of the papers on my desk,
 books and journals, graphs and tables, notes and analyses,
 the whole academic shebang: historicity, call, and response.
 The birdcage, I notice, is new, floor and metalwork spotless,
 though the little door swings free. "I'll tell you something else,"
 she says, smiles like she's enjoying herself, clips the little latch.
"Back to the drawing board with you. I didn't have any Kath."

FOUR
Domestic Service

THE BOARDINGHOUSE BEDROOM is brimsey brown and shiny from the hip down, so it reminds her of a conker from the chestnut tree back home. She wears the nightshift sewn by the fire in Glenavoo: her mother said what money they had was needed for a stout coat and boots.

Mrs. O'Meara, who runs the boardinghouse, seems to like her. Ellen thinks it because she doesn't have to jolly her up the way she does Anne Kerrigan, in the next room, who sobs, loud, at night and comes down puffy-eyed for breakfast and drains the good out of the day. If Ellen cries for home, it's quietly, and no one need tell her all will be dandy, just give it a little while.

After five days, with Mrs. O'Meara asking would she be needing the room next week, the Intelligence Office sends Ellen to be a kitchen maid in a tall house on Delancey Street. The first day, she is told to scrub the floor tiles in the kitchen and has to be shown how, never having needed to scrub the earthen floor at home. She kneels on an old cushion and cleans right into the corners, as she is told to do. She likes the shine of the gleaming tiles, their pattern in the clean light of the big window that Ann Reid, the cook, a bad-tempered woman from Roscommon, keeps open in all weathers so you can hear her curses in the yard if you're passing when she burns a loaf, which she hardly ever does.

The second day, Ellen breaks a glass and Ann Reid tells her she is stupid and clumsy, but wraps the shards in newspaper and says nothing to Miss Dowd, the housekeeper, a trim woman with a Kerry accent Ellen often can't make out. She calls the kettle "citil," and the doorbell "the bill," so Ellen thinks she is being told to get a piece of paper and opens the sideboard drawer. Ann laughs at her, but not too meanly, and explains how to be civil to callers and what to do with her hands.

Ellen has a small room at the top of the house, just wide enough for a bed and a table for the pitcher and ewer, but that is all she needs. She has never had a room of her own, and though she still misses home, of course she does, she likes having the span of the bed to kick and stretch as she sees fit, in the sliver of time between the knock at 5 a.m. and getting up and washed and ready to start cleaning the stairs at half past, not a second later, apron on, hair tidy, face and hands washed, like a good girl.

Mrs. West calls her Biddy when she passes her on the stairs and, for a second, Ellen thinks she is confusing her with another girl. Mrs. West has a baby, Harold, a six-month-old Ellen hears crying in the dead of night. She would like to help with him as she used to help with the babies at home but the baby has his own nurse, an English nurse: Ellen is not permitted to talk to him, either because it would distract her from her duties or because they're worried he might sound like she does, when he finally speaks. Even her peek-a-boo while she was cleaning out the ashes in the nursery grate meant he was carried to the window so his face was turned away.

Even a little baby, she thinks, is above her here.

FOR A COHORT REQUIRED TO BE LARGELY OUT OF SIGHT, there's any amount of material available on domestic servants in New York. Not on the servants themselves, of course, but on the idea of them; the finding of them, the cost, the managing, and the "problem" of them.

It was a topic that exercised all kinds of women in all kinds of print formats—society wives, magazine editors, etiquette arbiters, educators, social reformers, pamphleteers, fledgling sociologists.

Millions of words, I think it's fair to say, have been pressed to the service of the "Servant Question." Several contemporary historians, reclaiming women's lives as fit subject for study, give me the wherewithal to build a composite picture of the daily lives of women such as Ellen, allowing me to project what I think is a fair sense of the structure of their days, what's asked of them, what's forbidden to them, the demands and restrictions they lived within, and the pleasures snatched and reported back in their letters home.

At no other point in my research does the possible personage of Ellen O'Hara come into clearer view.

And at no other point does her voice flow more freely, like fresh water skittering in its riverbed over stone-cold facts and probabilities, over likelihood and proof.

Today I'm at my desk by 9 a.m. pleased to be eyeing the stack of books delivered to me yesterday for delving into today. My job will be to sift and pounce on the best details I can find to bring her day to life.

"Soft work, so," I imagine her saying to me. "'Tis very easy for some."

And once I hear her say this much, I can't help but hear her say more.

"At Mr. Bishop's Intelligence Office, I told a woman in spectacles
I could keep hens, kill a pig, lift potatoes, mind children if I had to,
though I'd rather not. She asked had I worked in a 'respectable'
household, so I said yes, thinking of home. She asked could I sew,
polish a floor, black a stove, carry a tray, and I said yes to the lot,
thinking it was no class of a lie, as maybe I could, if I hadn't yet.
She inspected my hands, wrote 'clean' clear as day, handed back
Father Moran's letter like it had fleas, copied only 'Good to work.'

"The girl waiting beside me asked me where I was from, in Irish,
nearly cried when I told her, for she herself was from Westport.
The woman in spectacles told her to return when she had shoes
but the girl had no money, she said, for shoes. I often wondered
what came of her, the barefoot girl, if she got a position even so.
I was sent to Mrs. West on Delancey and she wasn't, is all I know."

"I worked for doctors, merchants, bankers, a war widow.
 If it had been a case of the richer the house, the kinder
 the family, I'd have noticed, believe me. It was rarely so.
 You'd go on your first day, from the agency, and either
 you'd be offered tea while the house was explained to you
 or you'd not, and you'd know from the off what to expect,
 cold cuts in winter, no callers allowed, no stove in your room
 and a mistress you couldn't satisfy, overly keen to inspect
 the fold of sheets, the napkin darn, the softness of the bread.

"Some houses were better: one had a hand-pump and boiler
 for laundry. One had a boy to lug the coal. One, a comfy bed.
 One had shamrocks on maids' aprons. One had us call her
 'Your Ladyship.' She played the piano for visitors and sang
 'The Last Rose of Summer' and 'She Is Far from the Land.'"

Kitchen of the Merchant's House Museum, New York City. Photo by Max Touhey, 2018. Image courtesy of the Merchant's House Museum, 29 East Fourth Street, New York.

"I'd never trust a mistress to be as civil as she seemed:
  cross one or ever answer back, you'd see a different side.
  Break one of her precious china plates, she'd fire you
  with no reference, and take the plate out of your pay.
  One Biddy just as good as the next, I suppose, not a lick
  between us: ignorant, every one of us, barely civilized
  (hardly surprising; sure weren't we all reared in pigsties?).
  We smelled, had no manners—worst of all, were Catholic.

"I had my own rules for getting by: make Cook into a friend.
  If there were children in the house, don't get too fond.
  Curse only in Irish; bless myself to make it seem a prayer.
  Look right at anyone speaking to me, mistress or master.
  And when the loneliness came over me heavy in bed,
  dig my fingernail into my palm, but stop before it bled."

"The worst job was chamber pots, the smell of them first thing,
always the newest girl's job to take them out back for emptying.
Next worst was laundry, sleeves and collars scrubbed in the sink
until your fingers stung with cold and your wrists flopped weak.
If it rained, we'd hang the wet sheets on the rafters in our rooms
where they'd creak and shuffle and sag like old people at home.

"Best was when the mistress would leave us pretty much alone
while she fussed over callers or gossip or her quilling scenes
of an English hunt or Lords and Ladies at some a royal ball.
I'd have quilled them black and blue—hunts, dances, and all,
as I knew well how they'd come by their horses and gowns,
who went hungry for their silver shoe-buckles and fine wines.

"At least here, they paid us for labor; we were fed and warm,
and if airs and graces could be laughed at, they did little harm."

Though two-thirds of all women of working age in Ireland in 1901 had no wage-earning jobs, almost three-quarters of their sisters in the United States in 1900 were earning independent livelihoods.

—JANET A. NOLAN (1989, 69)

As late as 1900 60.5 percent of all Irish-born women who labored in the United States worked in domestic capacities.

—HASIA R. DINER (1983, 89)

As late as 1900 . . . over 40 percent of the nation's 320,000 servants were Irish-born.

—JAMES R. BARRETT (2012, 123)

Scene

You're in the drawing room on the last day of the month. Cook has warned you to keep your hands clean all morning, spick-and-span, no matter what job you're doing, for when he calls.

Mr. West is standing by the fireplace that isn't set and won't be lit for another month or two. How you'll fit the cleaning and setting into your morning's work is a bafflement, every minute already packed tight, this chore and that overlapping, like kittens in a heap.

You're not sure if you're allowed to look him in the eye, but, when he speaks, you do anyway and note he gives back no sign of offence.

"You've worked well this first month," he says. "Keep going and you'll soon get into the run of things."

The run of things? There's more?

He picks from the mantelpiece a bundle of notes already counted out. You wait until he extends them toward you before putting out your hand so it won't look like you're begging.

They're big, the notes, bigger than your hand, and the one on top has "$10" written on it and pictures either side that you can't make out from just looking down, so you put them in your apron pocket, say "Thank you" and add nothing more. And when he doesn't either, you slightly bow (only your head, nothing south of your chin), and you turn for the door, your fingers touching the big notes in your pocket that have, you think, some kind of heat in them.

You run up to your bedroom for the two minutes you have, lay them out around you on the bed. This afternoon, you'll go with Cook to the Savings Bank, it being the servants' half-day. She'll show you, she's promised, how to open a savings account and to pay into it, and how to ask for a money order to send home, when you've got put enough by.

In Glenavoo they'll turn your money order back into cash, smaller notes with "Bank of England" on them, notes that will rest for a short time only in the hands of Glenavoo.

You don't understand how any one piece of paper can change and change again, country to country, dollar to pound, having crossed the ocean you crossed but backward, losing nothing at all in the process, and being worth the very same.

"Help Wanted, Females": *New York Herald*, January 17, 1891. Image courtesy of the Library of Congress, Prints and Photographs Division, Washington, DC. *www.loc.gov/item/sn83030313/1891-01-17/ed-1*.

Scene

There's a row of bells in the hall, fourteen of them, each with a number you've to memorize so you know who's summoning you. No. 1 is the front door, that's easy. No. 2 is the drawing room. No. 3 is the master's bedroom, and No. 4 is the mistress's. So many rooms, each with a fire to be tended. Each with shelves of gew-gaws to be dusted, and better not break anything.

This morning, when you're cleaning the nursery, you step on a toy soldier, hear it snap. Luckily, Nurse has taken the baby out to the park and you're alone in the room. It's easy to place the two pieces under a corner of the rug where Nurse will make the same mistake but won't be able to curse because of the baby in earshot. Let her pay, you think: she's haughty. And she earns more.

There's a whole boxful of wooden soldiers and there's only one Ellen. One Nurse too, but she is from London and earns three times what you earn, and doesn't care who knows it.

Nurse will do just what you've done, of course; she'll hide the broken toy. And you'll enjoy knowing that, despite her shiny accent that has no soil or stones in it, she's like you, after all, fonder of wages than she is of toy soldiers that a baby can't play with.

Scene

It's your afternoon off and you've walked to Ladies' Mile, as you do every week for an hour or so, to do what Ann Reid calls your "window shopping." Macy's has a Christmas display, fancy gowns of green and red. Fur stoles and muffs. Hats with feathers you know are ostrich because the label says so.

You're used to homemade: shop-bought in Glenavoo was for emigrating. And you're used to sewing what needs to be sewn—plain work, darning and turning collars, no need for embroidery. At home, your mother and sisters and you would sit close in to the fire, a nice quietness to the room broken only by the draw of thread and a flutter of chat now and then.

You've your eye on a soft-collared coat with big cream buttons down the front and one on each cuff too. You think if you could ever afford this coat, you could give the sturdy one your mother bought you to the woman in the park with no coat at all, who is mumbling what sounds like Irish words whenever you walk by.

But how could you save enough for this coat, even if, as Ann Reid promises, there will be discounts in the stores? Every penny spent on a coat would be a penny rightly put to a fare for a passage here for Bridget or Annie.

Maybe a dress, if not a coat? Maybe stockings, if not a dress? Maybe a paste brooch to liven up the coat from home? Or maybe a run of fabric you could make into a blouse, your head bent over your work at night, your stitching hand rhyming with the stitching hand of your mother in Glenavoo?

The most important occupation for women was domestic or personal services. Live-in jobs solved housing problems for single women, which were acute in the big cities.

—PAULINE JACKSON (1984, 1007)

To single Irish women, domestic service meant comfortable living quarters, nourishing food, clean clothing, a taste of civilized living, and, in view of the room and board, offered better pay than work in a factory, mill, or the garment industry.

—LAWRENCE J. MCCAFFREY, IN BAYOR AND MEAGHER (1996, 217)

"Members of the Monaghan Men's Irish Dancing Class and Their Partners," ca. 1905. Image courtesy of the Library of Congress, Prints and Photographs Division, Washington, DC.

Scene

Still, when you walk through Washington Market, you don't know what to make of it. Vegetables with a strange color, like they've a temper on them. Fruit that isn't berries plucked from hedges when summer wanes. The meat cuts look more or less the same, but you've no need to buy meat.

You could count on two hands the plain food of Glenavoo: vegetables from your kitchen garden, rashers for a feast, porridge, bread baked in a skillet, eggs when the hens allowed. Here you don't even have names for most of what you see and when you do, they're strange: hazelnuts are filberts; broth is *boo-lawn*. Oysters are heaven knows what.

But you've learned that watermelon isn't turnip and that shallots in stew are not eyeballs.

Michael from Swinford is at the fruit stall today and he gives you a small, knobbly orange. You'll take it straight up to your room, peel it like he showed you how, and eat it as if it were a secret, and a good secret too. Every time after when you eat an orange you'll think of that first taste of it, how you thought at once you'd not want to live a life again with no oranges in it.

An 1890s Massachusetts survey set the servant's average work week at about 85 hours. . . . The day usually started by 6 am and ended no earlier than 7 pm. Many servants were then on call to answer the door or serve guests.

—JAMES R. BARRETT (2012, 123)

Servants worked seven days a week. Time off was usually limited to one afternoon and one night, per week, usually Sunday and Thursday.

—MARGARET LYNCH-BRENNAN (2009, 104)

Manny a night I don't even feel like writing home. Tis work work all the time.

—KATIE O'SULLIVAN, SAN JOSE, CALIFORNIA, TO HER BROTHER IN KERRY, IRELAND, DECEMBER 5, 1906, QUOTED IN MILLER (2008, 319)

AFTERNOONS OFF WOULD HAVE BEEN, I'm sure, for writing letters home; for scraping together news that wasn't all about work, work, work (for who at home would want to hear about the drudgery?). You'd say you were content and well, that you'd landed on your feet. That the family you were with was generous and took care to treat you kindly (whether they did or not). You'd leave out accidents or illness, not to disquiet them. Nothing about loneliness in your heart like a thorn. Or the dream you had of walking by the shore of Lough Talt. Nothing about the longing, or the want of being home.

Into the envelope with the letter went the bank order, and that was it then, for a while, the length and breadth of the cord connecting you with home. Until the next letter would come with news of all well, thank God, the weather promised fine, the new calf hale and the turf all saved.

Into the envelope went the bank order so no one would say you'd sent an empty letter, empty but for words.

You'd hardly trust the words yourself and you'd wonder about them at home, if they polished up the news the same way you did, if all was smooth and easy as they said, or if there was trouble on the farm, fields flooded and hay ruined, the hens slack or the rent due soon.

When the letter would come for you, your name written neat and true in your father's hand, you'd slip it in your apron pocket and carry it with you through the rooms, the knowledge of it like a magic trick to make the day pass quickly until you'd get a quiet hour to read it quietly.

"They paid me the month in dollar bills, two quarters, a luck-penny.
 For the first time in my life I learned to make friends with money.
 I slept on my bills, a clever sleep, to wish them ten bills more;
 the penny, I sewed in my apron lest I'd forget why I came here.
 At the Savings Bank, five dollars bought an order for a pound
 for the rent back home. Once that was sent, we'd set aside
 a little, by and by, for a hat or dress. Who wants to be serving
 six days a week, and still look like a servant on day seven?

"Did I mind? That money I skivvied for should slip through
 my father's open hands, God bless him, into the greedy maw
 of a landlord who'd demand every farthing owed, good harvest
 or bad, no matter if a man was sick or if his children starved?
 My seven days a week hard labor—grime and ash and slack-
 converted to carriages, jewels and law. That's some magic trick."

Eight out of every ten who send money home are girls.

—D. W. CAHILL, *CATHOLIC TELEGRAPH*, MARCH 16, 1861

The widow of a laborer remembered a sister of hers who had emigrated . . . and after four weeks sent home one pound. In Ireland, she commented, her sister would have had to work three months to earn an equal amount.

—ARNOLD SCHRIER (1958, 111)

THREE GENERATIONS DOWN, I WOULD BE, I suppose, unimaginable to her, full days sitting at a computer screen, breaking only to stretch my legs along marble corridors, or to make myself tea.

Unimaginable, my freedoms. Unimaginable, my work.

Hard work, Ellen's, for long hours of a week she had little governance of.

Hers to do what she was bid; mine to do my own bidding.

Hers to work thirteen hours a day; mine to think about that work, how hard it must have been.

Hers to depend on her legs, her back, for her livelihood.

Mine to fashion a clump of shadow into her guiding hand.

The thought, sallow and silvered, is the kind of mirror you learn to avoid whenever you walk by a certain wall on low afternoons.

But I want my work to rhyme with hers, my life and hers to be locked in a structure that flexes around both of us: her life and my telling of it linked by a form, centuries old, that pairs sounds and orders time and seeps into a thrown voice.

That's how I justify the way I'm allowed to call this *work*.

Today, you sit on your chair, as usual, but don't speak.
Instead, you look at the pages of printouts, pick up a book
on Irish servants and flick through; you don't seem impressed.
You stop at a cartoon from Puck that has the mistress
of the house browbeaten by a slovenly Irish cook
with a monkey face. I'm surprised to see you smirk.
Next is a page of newspaper classifieds: "Americans Only,"
"We Seek a Protestant Girl," or "No Irish Need Apply."

No smiles now. You slap shut the book, shake your head,
pause for a moment, then open it at random to a spread
with the heading "The Uppishness of the Irish Bridget,"
then put the book, very definitely, down. Yes, stupid
is what they took you for: primitive, superstitious, naïve,
and stubborn. (Of which last your being here is proof?)"

"How Biddy Served Tomatoes Undressed." *"Indade ma'am an I'll not take off another STITCH if I loose me place."* Benjamin West Kilburn, 1892, Albumen silver print, 84.XC.979.5087. J. Paul Getty Museum, Los Angeles, Gift of Weston J. and Mary M. Naef.

"Indeed, we came in for more than our fair share of abuse.
We were easy prey, the butt of the jokes, as not many of us
had the wherewithal to show them up in all their foolery.
But we weren't as stupid as they thought: we had schooling,
most of us—could write and read and tally sums, and in two
languages, like as not, which is more than they could do.
Not for us, hours of quilling or fussing over a dinner menu,
spending today calling on who tomorrow would call on you.

"If I'd had half their money I'd have got more joy of it
than the foolish sniggering they inclined to take for wit.
With more jobs than maids being usual, we had our pick;
no need to suffer either sniggering mistress or bad cook.
For us to do the work their kind would never deign to do,
they had to pay over the odds. Which we thought funny too."

My Biddy

From rosy morning to dewy eve,
who is it makes my soul to grieve,
and after all doth take French leave?
> *My Biddy.*

Who roasts my meat into a coal,
Who breaks my nicest china bowl,
and says she "didn't on her sowl"?
> *My Biddy.*

Who polishes the kitchen floor,
and in half an hour or more
has it precisely as before?
> *My Biddy.*

My pocket handkerchiefs and hose,
who confiscates under the rose,
and wears by turns my nicest clothes?
> *My Biddy.*

Who comes and goes whene'er she chooses,
injures whatever thing she uses,
and now and then to work refuses?
> *My Biddy.*

Who slams, and bangs, and breaks, and smashes,
who tears, and rends, and knocks, and dashes,
who tips, and spills, and slops, and splashes?
> *My Biddy.*

And shall I ever cease to be
in bondage unto such as thee?
My way is dark—I can not see.
> *For Biddy.*

I only know my misery;
I only wish thee over the sea;
I only wish that I were free.
> *From Biddy.*

—FROM *THE DAYS' DOINGS*, APRIL 17, 1869

"The Irish Declaration of Independence That We Are All Familiar With," *Puck*, May 9, 1883.

"None of us stayed in one place long, though they'd offer
  small extras for us to stay put: use of a room for callers,
  a carriage to Mass on wet Sundays, an allowance of tea,
  the Mistress's cast-off dress, gifted with much ceremony.
  A paid week off got to be normal or, if you were sick,
  a doctor called without you having to have his fee docked.

"But what cared I for sitting-rooms or dresses or gewgaws?
  I'd move for a dollar more a month. Or stay for a dollar raise.

"Nights off were merciful release. Best was a Sligo Society dance
  where you'd catch up with cousins and such, with the chance
  of being introduced to a half-decent man (if there's such a thing.
  Though Maggie, Bridget, Sally, and Annie did fine, considering).

"I left it late: a husband would have stopped the money home.
  By the time I could entertain it, the best I could do was John."

FIVE

John

TODAY I PILE COAT and bag and scarf up on your wooden chair: I am forestalling you. I don't quite want to stop you in your stride (not when you're telling me, so nicely, everything) by announcing that I've not been able to keep my part of the bargain. I've lost you.

Or, rather, from when you step off the *City of Berlin* in July 1882 right up until 1898, I have failed to find you, specifically and exactly, in any official record of the time.

You arrived too late for the 1880 census. Perhaps the 1890 federal census caught you beautifully, aged twenty-eight, in the prime of your life, employed, literate, single, and independent, but I'll never know. On January 10, 1921, the records of the 1890 census were, for the most part, destroyed by fire in the Department of Commerce building where they were housed in Washington, DC. Records not burnt in the fire (as the *News Journal* reported on January 11, 1921) "were submerged in water thrown into the basement of the building by more than twenty lines of hose which brought the conflagration under control." The report continues, "There are no duplicates of the destroyed records and the loss was declared probably the worst of its kind in the government's history."

I would find it hard to tell you that all trace of your young self was either lost in fire or drowned in feet of water, you who sailed an ocean to come here.

FEDERAL CENSUS RECORDS FROM 1790 DESTROYED IN COMMERCE BUILDING FIRE

All Data On Decennial Enumerations Up To 1910 Are Lost When Flames Sweep Government Building.

FILES FOR 1920 ARE SAVED

Blaze Originates In Basement Where Papers Were Stored---Water Poured Into Vaults Completes Damage---No Duplicates Of Documents Which Can't Be Replaced.
Three Firemen Overcome.

Washington, Jan. 10.—Priceless census records, dating back to 1790, when the first enumeration of the United States was taken, were destroyed tonight in a fire of undetermined origin at the Department of Commerce, Nineteenth street and Pennsylvania avenue. The records included figures from every census up to the present one, and officials said that it would be days before even an estimate of the damage could be given.

The blaze originated in the basement of the Commerce Building, and five alarms quickly brought every piece of apparatus in downtown Washington to the scene, and more than 20 lines of hose completed the damage done to the records by pouring tons of water through windows into vaults where the records were kept.

THREE FIREMEN ARE OVERCOME

Census fire report, *Baltimore Sun*, January 11, 1921, 1.

THERE ARE ALWAYS OTHER RECORDS, other proofs. Here's one: the fact of me. And of my mother, and of hers.

From life, from my mother, I know Ellen married John Grady and they had two children, James and Anna (Annie), my grandmother.

But who was John?

I go rummaging.

The *New Rochelle Pioneer* lists in its "Advertised Letters" section an unclaimed letter addressed to John Grady, lying in the post office in May 1896.

Was it to him?

Did he ever go in to claim it, I wonder, or was it discarded after a certain time, burned, no doubt, with all the other orphaned letters of the time?

(Imagine if the twenty-nine letters itemized in this advertisement were to exist still, to be opened and read at last, like a magnifying glass held to so many lives otherwise lost to us!)

ADVERTISED LETTERS,

The following are the list of unclaimed letters remaining in the New Rochelle Post Office for week ending May 23d, 1896.

LADIES' LIST.

Mrs Mabberday	Mrs Alden P Webster
Mrs White	Bessie Blomberg
Miss Ida Gauffin	Miss B Hunter
Miss N May	Miss Mary Morgan
Miss Mao Carthy	Miss M E MacCarthy
Miss Josie Murray	Miss Bessie Manly

GENTS' LIST.

H S Allison	Fred Barker
H Barr	John Grady
L Gromlach	George Happon
James Harrison	Paul Engle
E M Lockwood	Antonio Powazzo
Mr Renold	W J Robinson
Adolph Schwonger	John H Turner

FOREIGN.

Helen M Graves	Tilda Nilsson
Ann Smith	

In calling for the above letters please say "advertised."   W. V. Morron, P. M.

Advertised letters, the *New Rochelle Pioneer*, May 23, 1896, 8.

I RECEIVE A NEW ROCHELLE LETTER OF MY OWN, from the city clerk's office: Ellen and John's marriage certificate—the first definite, incontrovertible trace since the record of your baptism, back in 1862.

Typically, your name is misgiven. For this document only, you are Ellen G. Hara, whose marriage to John Grady (Carpenter) on January 9, 1898, was officiated by Reverend R. B. Cushion, according to Record No. 545.

Just over nine months later, Jimmy is born, and the following year, in October 1899, comes Annie.

And here you are again, my Ellen, cornered in the census return of 1900 (June 11), with your family at 92 Drake Avenue, New Rochelle.

You are listed as "Ellinor." At first I think it can't be you. But one of the surprising things about archival research is that sometimes, just sometimes, it unfurls, obligingly, toward (not away from) you.

I expect there to be other families of just two children called James and Anna Grady. There aren't any other such families: there's only one.

This, finally, must be you.

John is listed as head of household and trolley motorman, born in New York in 1869, which makes him seven years younger than you. (I think I see why you gave your year of birth as 1870, knocking a clean eight years off your age.)

John can read, write, and speak English.

And that's the last we'll hear of him.

He takes himself off-record, either into doughy New York soil, or the blue yonder of God knows where.

Ellen, Elin, Ellinor, Ella, Ellie, Hillin: you were all. (Or some. Or one.)

You slipped between names like you slipped between countries. Between being there, foursquare, in the record, and being untraceable, to me.

Of course, I cannot pin you down: you'd smirk at the idea. (Or your ghost would.)

What I'm after is certainty; what I have is guesswork and approximation.

One story as good as another, perhaps, when you can't be sure of the truth.

While I'm delighted to find you, of course, I also feel something contrary—a small prurience, perhaps, as though I'm witnessing a private occasion: a contractual moment between your small family and the vast, impartial machinery of state. I'm not sure how to describe myself in relation to this moment—not bystander, witness, or bit-part player, I am so far after the fact that the facts are able to ignore my watching them perform there.

I am an irrelevance.

But I can't leave it there.

Is it vanity, this impulse to wield my synthesizing, dramatizing hand? Is imagining the occasion an act of inexcusable appropriation or of forgivable curiosity?

Is wanting to animate their lives, so otherwise beyond me, a brazen, narcissistic impulse, or is it somehow serviceable? Is there a way to make it be both?

I decide to write the scene, to permit myself, and then to rake over what I write in your tined, resistant voice.

I am as the census enumerator, spacebar and cursor for form and pen, pinning down one version of you this New York afternoon.

Because a census gathers names together and then gets personal, I imagine the filling of it as a kind of intimate occasion. A family gathered around a table, serious about the official task of accounting for themselves to the enumerator. Ellen has made a cake, and has taken off her apron for Mr. Aster's call.

I imagine lots.

I put John down for being every inch the sober household head. And the children have to be there too, though they are small and

U.S. Census Bureau record for the O'Grady family (sixth from the top). Year: 1900; census place: New Rochelle, Ward 2, Westchester, New York; page: 11; enumeration district: 0094; FHL microfilm: 1241176, New York Public Library.

have no sense of the world and how they might fit into it. I allow John to take charge, to answer the dates when he's sure of the answer, to channel the questions to Ellen when he's not. Ellen has all the dates lined up (especially the one requiring practice, if it's to sound plausible).

I set them down in a kind of pride in the fact of being there, of being written officially down.

For all I know, Mr. Aster called to the door one afternoon when John was on the trolleys, and James was wanting to go out and kept fetching his little boots, and the baby was fussing and Ellen distracted, so she fired off the names and dates as if it hardly mattered that the occupants of 92 Drake Avenue, New Rochelle, had a claim on being recognized for the family they had so recently become.

But I fill in my own record of this recording as significant: ritualized, as nothing else about these four people together will be again.

That census entry of 1900 is the one and only time this family appears, recognizably, in the record, together.

FIRST COMES THE FACT, then the imagination wanting to occupy that fact. Then the reckoning the space between them, the excuses and qualifications, the claw-back.

From which arises your voice now, skeptical, self-possessed; in possession of truths unknown to me and keen to let me know it. Also, resistant to my supposings. Also, in high dudgeon at the barefaced cheek of me.

"Dear God, is there to be no end of imagining this day?
The thing about raking over old ground, as they say,
is that not everything turned up, you'd want to keep.
And mind you don't trip over it, this treasure trove
of tittle-tattle you keep adding to. There might be traps,
dead ends and whatnot, you might not get back out of,
places you'd get stuck forever, worrying your little head
about rights or wrongs, ins and outs of anything I've said.

"Is it not a great deal of time and energy to lavish on a life
that isn't yours? Where's your husband, your own children,
that you have time to ask so many questions about mine?
The devil, you know, makes work for idle hands, and yours
look plenty idle from where I sit today. Do you not have
something better, pray tell, to be doing with these hours?"

Many of the Irish women who listed themselves as "widows" may really have been abandoned wives too proud to admit it, finding it somewhat more respectable and sympathetic to be in the role of the bereaved.
—HASIA R. DINER (1983, 59)

Rates of widowhood and male absence or desertion were notably higher among the Irish in America than in Ireland, so that a disproportionately high number of Irish women found themselves single and economically self-sufficient in America.
—KEVIN KENNY (2000, 151)

JOHN GRADY. All I have of him for sure is his 1898 marriage certificate and that 1900 census return, as though the camera has been out of focus for thirty years and suddenly snaps into a vision so acute it cannot be sustained and so slips out of focus again.

No birth certificate, no death certificate. As disappearing tricks go, it's convincing. John Grady has well and truly hidden himself: a slippery customer, through and through. I wonder what Ellen saw in him. True, she was already well over thirty when she married; maybe he was the best she could do in the time she had. And maybe, if you're going to lie about your age, you need an audience that's maybe a little wanton itself, betimes, about the truth.

Maybe she loved him.

If she did, she must have been disappointed. He was not a solid proposition. I can't pin him down, this John Grady who marries my great-grandmother, fathers two children by her, then simply disappears. I don't know where he went; could be Seattle, could be Swinford, who knows?

My mother told me her maternal grandfather was shot and killed one morning while working on the subway. Her sister-in-law said that was hooey, and that he'd taken off. My mother was keen on respectability, and wasn't above enjoying embellishing a story with entirely plausible and wonderfully vivid illustrative detail. My child's imagination, I recall, latched on to the terrible murder with the full force of a credulous innocence fully prepared to leaven a somewhat routine rural life in midlands Ireland with the dark glamour and drama of a New York morning, blood spilling from a body slumped on a tiled and footfalled floor.

The murderer, I recall my mother telling me, got clean away.

No John Grady, that I can find, died in New Rochelle in 1900 or 1901. And I can find no record of any such murder in the newspapers of the day.

John Grady is a dead end.

Or maybe I'm just not trying hard enough. Maybe I don't want to.

Because what happens next in this story is that John becomes a shadow, a mysterious name, a hollow name, called on when it is useful to Ellen and, otherwise, consigned to darkness. Where, I suspect, it rightly belongs.

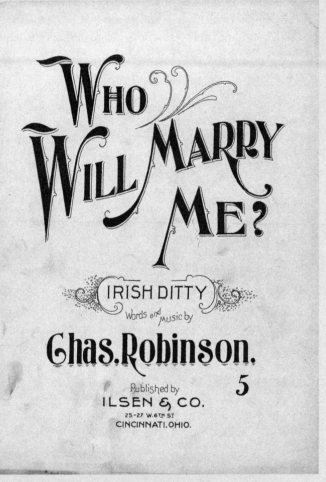

IT SEEMS INDECOROUS TO ASK a ghost why she chose the man she did.

Why does anyone, when it comes down to it?

It is a dark, sleety February day. My office is full of shadows this morning, uncowed by any lamp. The corner where your chair stands is fretted by pewter light. You could be there in all your wool and skin, and I'd barely make you out.

If you were, I know you'd now be looking straight into my eyes. Anything I'd say to you, you'd throw right back at me, and you'd be right to. There's no question I could put to you I haven't asked myself a hundred times.

Did I find answers?

Oh, you know.

Only a kind of smothering answer: I chose him because I wanted to, and I hadn't any reason (then) to ram a needle in that want to puncture it.

He gave me two children and maybe the good of them canceled the bad of him.

Is this how we account for ourselves, the good and the bad tallied and checked, topped and tailed, skimmed and squished in all together, until everything comes out someway even, like the household ledger of a daintily kept house?

Here is my hand, busy with you, writing down and rubbing out. And writing down again.

"Have you ever thought you might be barking up the wrong tree?
  Maybe it was me left John, upped one day and away off with me,
  enough of his drinking and shenanigans to last an entire life?
  What say you now? What will you make of this possible swerve,
  who makes a spiral of every turn, straightens them out into lists?
  In your telling of the life I lived, how would you account for this?
  You'll never know, is the eat and drink of it, the pip and skin.
  I could tell you this or tell you that. I could tell you anything.

"And you'd just take it, sit there at your desk, tipping away
  like you're bouncing small coins off my back, or tapping
  a finger hole in my forehead, or knocking on my coffin lid.
  Here's a story: write it down as true. Now here's the opposite.
  He left me. Or I left him. What does it matter to you, anyway,
  who spends her days, that I can see, not living but typing?"

SIX

Returning I

SEPTEMBER 1901. You've been in America for nineteen years, your life recently caught in an upswing of marriage and family.

Until it wasn't.

One of two things, from what I can make out, is going to happen now.

1. You and your sturdy, ambitious husband decide it would be best all round for you to take your two children back to your parents in Sligo and leave them there for a bit. That'll give you both, he says, a chance to work and line your nest, give them a proper home. (Or has he recently lost his job, is finding it hard to get back on his feet?)

or

2. John upped and is gone, leaving you with two excitable toddlers in a town where none of your relatives live, and no help available. So you do what young women sometimes do, with their backs against the wall. You go home to your parents. And bring your children with you. And sometime during the visit, you decide to leave them there.

I know which one seems likelier, which one I believe to be true.

Either way, what we have now is three passengers sailing on September 28, New York to Queenstown, on the RMS *Etruria*. And only one of them, Ellen, sailing back on the SS *Umbria* on October 27.

Three weeks to travel up to Sligo and back south.

Three weeks to take and leave your children.

Then back to New York alone, nothing but work ahead of you.

"Yes, I left them where they'd be safe and well cared for, with my family,
    which was also their family—my parents, James, John, and young Sally.
    Room made for them. My mother delighted, so many of hers gone,
    and father, forever dandling Jimmy as he'd rarely done his sons.
    They were better off. I'd no job or husband, two babies in New York,
    no money for rent and no one to look after them if I did find work.
    Not able to pass myself off as a widow there, with no death certificate
    and no softness in the place, no forgiveness, no support.

"So, yes, we went home, the three of us, and brought a tragic story
    of my unfortunate, darling husband shot during a robbery.
    To save scandal, my mother knew the truth, and no one else.
    My crying done by night in my childhood bed, for even a loss
    not worth the mourning has to be mourned all the same.
    For the children's sake, though it chafed me, I kept his name."

. . . AND TOOK IT WITH YOU three weeks on, when you went back alone.

Oh, Ellen Grady with your carpetbag and your children left behind. I follow you on deck, your face set to a future that could go any which way, no knowing for sure you would get them back or make a go of it.

. . . and, on the voyage, thinking of them waking to her, gone, these past three days.

. . . and thinking the storm that blew up on day five wasn't half the match of the storm inside her head.

. . . and thinking every mouthful of food would lodge in her throat, so she could die before she'd make land.

. . . and thinking of them going to sleep in her absence, this night and every single night to come.

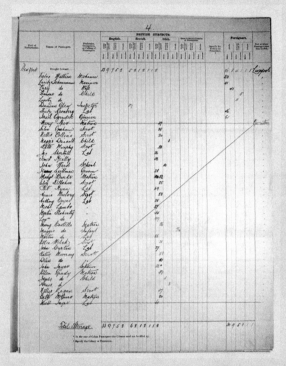

Passenger manifest of the RMS *Etruria*. Ellen, James, and Annie are sixth, fifth, and fourth from the bottom. UK and Ireland, incoming passenger lists, 1878–1960, www.Ancestry.com, 2008.

"SS *Umbria* Departing for New York from Liverpool," 1902, H. C. & Co. White. Image courtesy of the Rijksmuseum, Amsterdam.

ON THE MANIFEST OF THE *Umbria* her name is last on the
page, and misspelled, Gready. (This strikes me as apt: it wasn't
her name and maybe didn't quite sit easily on her, with her
husband, who owned it, gone.) Her age is given as forty (in fact,
she was thirty-nine—the single time I've found her age revised
upward, instead of downsized to fit). Otherwise, it lists her as
"housekeeper," able to read and write and (intriguingly), not a
polygamist. Her mental and physical health are both good; she is
not, apparently, deformed or crippled (the last column), has paid
her own passage, and has twenty dollars in cash in her possession.
(In comparison, Annie Magner from Cork, heading to service
in New York, has three dollars, and John Gannon, laborer, from
Tullamore, returning to his aunt on West 39th Street in New York,
has sixty dollars.)

The page has been damaged over time, the bottom curled up
so there are words about her I can't read. Her last residence, for
example, is illegible.

But what's clear is that in the column headed "Whether Going
to Join a Relative and If So, What Relative, Their Name and
Address," Ellen has said that she is bound for New Rochelle where
her husband, John, awaits her return at 92 Drake Avenue.

Which gives credence, perhaps to Option 1. But I still don't
go for it.

She gave, I'm guessing, whatever facts would get her through
New York immigration with fewest riddling questions asked, least
chance of saying the wrong thing. Less risk of slipping up.

ON THE *ETRURIA*, you were neatly accounted for—Ellen, Jimmy, and Annie: your name spelled right, the page presented clean and orderly. On the *Umbria*, returning alone, the passenger list is disrupted and damaged. And your name is Ellen Gready, though the address is yours. It looks as though the ledger has been scorched, the bottom margin curling up so your record is incomplete. You are fudged.

For once, the record tells more than it knows, and tells it beautifully.

Part of you is missing, that is all.

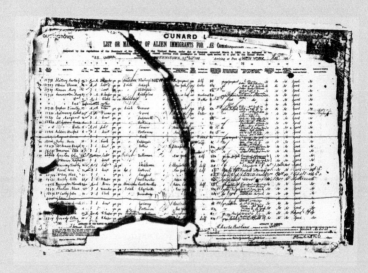

Passenger manifest for the SS *Umbria*. Ellen's entry is last on the page. Arrival: New York, New York; microfilm serial: T715, 1897–1957; line: 30; page number: 76, *Passenger Lists of Vessels Arriving at New York, New York, 1820–1897*. Year: 1901. Records of the U.S. Customs Service, Record Group 36. National Archives, Washington, DC.

THIS MORNING A BUSKER PLAYS under my window on Fifth Avenue, sassy Latin tunes to shake out a few busy pockets, and then, once the morning rush is over, he slows it down to a tender song, though I don't understand the words: could be love, could be homesickness, could be a mourning song. People, I see, are listening (as I am) to his song laying down its lacquer on the city day.

When I look over, your head is down as if you're listening too. Once, you nod. You don't look up until it's over and he's back to giddy, good-time tunes, tunes with their sunny side out.

Strange, the ways we find to get back home. You, for one: the set of your shoulders is the very same as my mother's, all those years ago; and your voice, when I find it, is crosshatched with identical darkness.

I think I know you.

The words, which I will call—for the sake of it—your words, fall into place like coins into an upturned hat or guitar case. I am busking you for all you are worth: I won't let you leave until I've emptied all your pockets; until I've cleaned you out.

But the words come willingly all the same: the tone secure and confident, the voice holding its own.

"Oh, I always knew I'd get them back. That was the plan,
 no doubting it, to leave them safe and sound with kin
 and came back here to work. I'd have stayed if I could,
 but Kavanagh told me to my face I was too old
 for a shopgirl, and a servant's wage over there
 was a pittance, an insult, compared with back here.
 So, I'd start over in New York, mind every cent,
 get work as a housemaid, live in, save on the rent.

"Three years, I reckoned, and I'd be in business
 with my own place, four bedrooms, two for us
 and two for young Irish men fresh off the boat
 in need of a mammy who'd cook them stirabout,
 make them write a letter home on Saturdays,
 and get them out on Sundays for first Mass."

"And so it was. Not exactly quite how I'd foreseen:
it took me much longer, for one thing, between
sending money home monthly for the extra mouths
and the first job I got after returning, having been out
of the way of service for some years, not being great,
Better than nothing, but barely even the best I could get.
The Rosenbergs paid only eight dollars a month, all in,
but I took it for the simple reason they had no children.

"I saved like a demon what I hadn't to send back home,
spent nothing on clothes, all my notions of fashion
put in a tin under my bed, quarter by quarter, dime
by dime. At the Savings Bank, they knew me by name
and learned not to sneer at my handful of small coins
that would build (it had to) our family home again."

"Three years I was there and never once said a word
　of Jimmy and Annie. Why would I? When other maids
　wanted to go to a fair or a dance, I'd stay back doing
　factory piecework, lacing up boots or plain sewing
　or extra laundry, anything to make my little tin sing
　its lullaby with the promise in it to my lost children.

"I was never not thinking of them both, believe me.
　All my prayers and plans went in their direction only.

"I darned torn curtains and sheets thought past repair.
　If a plate or cup was broken, I'd smuggle it upstairs
　and mend it best I could, stow it neatly in my trunk,
　pieced together a future out of what most call junk.
　Never stole a thing, mind, took only what was binned
　but steered it, always, toward that one, important end."

"On Jimmy's eighth birthday, Mrs. Dennehy found me crying
in the pantry, so I told her. She took me under her wing
taught me how to run a kitchen, little money-saving tricks,
how to boil bones for stock; always check the delivery box
for bad spuds and vegetables sneaked under the top layer.
Lard instead of butter. Sweet-talking tradesmen to ensure
you'd get a Christmas box. Saving carrot and potato skins
to flavor broth. A sharp knife to slice meat nice and thin.

"She'd let me take in laundry for doing, slyly, after hours
and never costed up the soap I used, or boiling water.
Her own son had died of fever on the ship coming over
and she swore she'd not see me lose even a day more
of my two than I had to. She was a dear friend to me
who hadn't many: close as, maybe closer, than family."

FAMILY. YOU HAD FAMILY IN AMERICA (who didn't?), just not quite the family of your own making or heart's desire.

Seven of the twelve O'Hara children sailed to America. As well as Ellen, Bridget, Anne, Kate, Michael, Maggie, and Sarah (Sally) went.

Six sisters and one brother left Aclare and lit out for America. Ellen, as we know, marries John Grady, bad cess to him. Bridget marries Patrick Welch in 1895, in Salem, Massachusetts. Annie marries Patrick J. Morgan (no relation to the banker) in New York in April 1908. Maggie marries John Doyle in the Church of the Blessed Sacrament in New York in February 1909. And Sally marries Thomas Landers in April 1912: they have two children, Thomas Jr. and Theresa, and live on West 60th Street.

I have no record of any marriage for Catherine or Cass or Cissie or Cal, or for any Katherine or Kate. Michael goes to California, shows up on a San Francisco voter registration form in 1904.

They scatter, as big families do, but Ellen, Annie, Maggie, and Sally all stick to New York.

Where they come to rely on each other, I'm guessing; where their children play with each other (but not Ellen's), and are kin.

Let's take a day in spring 1912, right before Sally marries Thomas. We have Ellen, Annie, Maggie, and Sally in New York. It should be easy to get them around a single table, maybe after Sunday Mass, with tea in the pot and a fresh loaf baked. Let's put Kate there too, and have Bridget travel down for Sally's wedding, and Michael, to give Sally away. The other men, the brothers-in-law, come and go. They know the clatter of these sisters, when they get together.

Ellen says, "Let's write a letter home. We'll take it in turns."

She has her own, separate letter written, to Jimmy and Annie. It will go in the same envelope.

And that's what they do, heads bent over the paper, rhyming with those other heads that will bend over the reading of it, back home. They take it in turns to write down bits and bobs of news. There is a page and there are lives to fill it and that is plenty, this spring day.

They write in English, as they were schooled to do, for all that Irish is the language of the kitchen in Glenavoo. The Irish that once fell from their tongues fell fast and flighty, as if it had the weather in it, a wind that could turn corners, a sun to riffle corn. But fall it did and kept on falling, between the cabin floorboards on the ships, down cracks in sidewalks, under stairs, between praying and talking, there and here, like change so small it was scarcely ever worth the searching for.

English is all their home now. English for writing, English for talking, English with different weather in it, street and crowds, no fields of corn or rain on the slant with a sideways lilt to it.

And so they write words with their bits of news, like blackberries first thing in the morning, with the light catching the dew.

That Maggie has knitted a green shawl.

That Kate sang "The Meeting of the Waters" on Saint Patrick's Day and, as usual, brought the house down.

And Bridget has read in the *New York Herald Tribune* that a man called Atwood is planning to fly from Newfoundland to Ireland, using the same path the big ships used, figures the trip will take just thirty hours.

And Ellen was nearly robbed on Fifth Avenue, only a lad saw what happened and chased the woman around the corner and got back her purse and nearly grabbed the quarter she offered him right out of her hand.

And Michael says he overheard two men talking Irish on a trolley car yesterday.

They all miss home and send their love. And hope to see everyone soon.

I expect you to throw me one of your looks, but you don't.

"There was no seeing everyone again: for us, that door had shut."
Home had two meanings, and also none. "First time I used it
for over here, I felt I'd sinned. You innocently put on your coat,
say, 'I'm for home', and hear yourself. And freeze. And realize.
Such a slippy, fickle word it is, butter-smothered. Or like ice.
Falls right out of your grasp." (Oh, yes, I also know it to be true
who has wriggled between countries, made a life of passing through.)

Other people's children. Husbands. Makeshift, stopgap homes.
"You do what you can, but half the time, you feel like you're alone
again on the ship coming over, no matter how many lives about you
or how busy you are, every day is another day to be gotten through.
I never had a notion of *home* without Jimmy and Annie there.
Wherever they were was my home too, be it New York or Aclare."

Census of Ireland, 1911. James and Anne Grady are both entered as "American" and as "scholar." Image courtesy of the National Archives of Ireland, NAI/CEN/1911/71/5.

You go a long, fallow stretch without them.

In the 1911 Irish census, they're still in Glenavoo, living with Austin and Anne and their uncle, James. They're both listed as "scholar," able to read and write, grandson and granddaughter, aged eleven and eight, respectively, both of them U.S-born.

On APRIL 30, 1912, James Francis Joseph Grady makes his Confirmation in Saint Attracta's Church. His address is given as Glenavoo and his parents listed as Ellen O'Hara and John Grady.

He's been there in Sligo for eleven years now.

It must feel like home, the only home they remember, to Jimmy and Annie both.

I TRAWL THROUGH THE U.S. IMMIGRATION RECORDS between 1901 and 1913, hoping to find an Ellen Grady (or even an Ellen O'Hara) who had returned home between times to see her children. There is none. I suppose she wouldn't spend the passage money when it was needed for the plan.

Which means that from the ages of three and two, respectively, until they were almost fifteen and fourteen, Jimmy and Annie did not see their mother. And she did not see them.

Twelve years of birthdays and Christmases, First Communions and Confirmations. Twelve years of only her handwriting and theirs, to stretch between them and her. And reports from their aunt and grandmother, their height, how they were doing at school, Jimmy so good around the farm, Annie's lovely chestnut hair.

AFTER THE *UMBRIA* IN 1901, your name goes dark for a long while. To find you I must listen only; my eyes are no good to me.

There are several possible Ellens in the 1905 New York census, but none of them quite fits into your outline. Wrong age, wrong husband, wrong children. One is a dressmaker. One has fourteen children. One is an inmate of the House for the Aged of the Little Sisters of the Poor.

None of them are you.

But in 1910 there's an Ellen Grady (forty), widowed, listed as a janitor, has two living children not with her on census night. She is the head of household, a wage earner with three boarders, Patrick Hurley, James Manning and John Moran, all living at 207 West 67th Street, Manhattan.

There you are, sturdy and solid in 1910, having pulled yourself up to head of household with three paying boarders on your books, your children in the wings.

You have made a life with room in it.

Not much longer now.

In September 1913, Jimmy and Annie sail back from Ireland to New York in the company of Mary Ann Barry and her son, William Henry, aged fifteen. A neighbor, maybe, or a cousin? The party of four is from Aclare, Co. Sligo. Anne and James are brother and sister, the ages are right, and, perhaps more tellingly, they are both listed as "Claiming U.S. Born." It has to be them—how many other U.S.-born children of correct name and age can be living in Aclare?

Mary Ann Barry, whoever she was, is listed as mother of William Henry and grandmother to James and Anne.

But she is not. She cannot be.

(Did anyone ever hand over true facts to the recorders of information on these transatlantic trips? Or was it a kind of free-for-all, a chance to invent or reinvent yourself, howsoever you saw fit?

God knows, the reality was plenty grim. I can understand why any woman of the time might want to give the facts a shaking, see if they settled, when they settled, any better way.)

They sail west. It must all seem new to them: they'd hardly remember the same journey twelve years earlier, going the other way.

They are children still, moving continents away from their home in Aclare, just as their mother had done.

But this time, someone is waiting for them, waiting like it's all she's been waiting for, the only point and purpose to her life. Waiting like the twelve years since she last saw them were a blur and inconvenience only: a personal suffering.

SHE HAS WAITED ALL THIS TIME TO SEE THEM, but I will make her wait a little longer.

How Ellen managed to construct a life is a story told by many Irish women in New York. Before I get Jimmy and Annie down from that ship, before her particular story picks up, I need to put her in a context of a general account.

Ellen was probably not more lucky or unlucky than most of us tend to be. John proved no great husband, it's true, but she, being resourceful, healthy, and determined, got past his abandonment and made a respectable family life without him anyhow.

Ellen managed what Irish women did in New York, if they could. She went from servant to head of household in her own boardinghouse.

Emigration got Ellen to New York, and emigration then fed her a stream of plucky lads in need of a home from home, glad of her accent and of anything familiar in her gait or face to remind them of mothers left behind, and to steady them in this strange new place that was nothing like they'd known.

Emigration translated Ellen from a backwater smallholding in Glenavoo to manager of her own business in Midtown.

Emigration made Ellen substantial: whatever losses it also involved, it distinguished her.

SEVEN

The Boardinghouse

YEARS OF SERVICE WOULD HAVE SCHOOLED YOU in the rote and rule of keeping house; in making do and eking out; in the useful shortcuts and the ones that backfire; in the recipes that double up at less than twice the price; in the tone to take with tradesmen; in how to settle bills. In how to be at beck and call, run ragged fifteen hours a day, clawed and bossed and pulled every which way, and still to be Ellen O'Hara from Glenavoo when you'd kneel down by your bed at night to pray for people who'd known to call you by a name that slipped right into theirs.

Call it progress: from the slights and demands of domestic service to the independence of your own boardinghouse. Call it betterment: the one version available to you with your thin education and nothing you could call capital—nothing to sell you could possibly sell and no one backing you.

Call it a career path in a world in which the term would have been unthinkable, for you.

Taking in boarders offered more independence . . . and it was in many places the only available employment for women who wanted to make money while staying at home to care for their children.
—SUSAN STRASSER (1982, 154)

Boardinghouses . . . ranged from the genteel to the seedy, and they formed a core institution in nineteenth-century New York. . . . Historians estimate that one-third to one-half of nineteenth-century urbanites lived in such lodgings.
—CINDY R. LOBEL (2014, 107)

Fifteen percent of all Irish-American households in 1900 earned income from an average of two lodgers housed in each.
—JANET A. NOLAN (1979, 79)

A WOMAN RUNNING A BOARDINGHOUSE had a degree of independence, her own income and more control over her day than any servant would.

Against that, she had financial responsibility: rent and monthly bills to settle, her income dependent on prompt and proper payment from young men whose own income was quite likely precarious, if they were laborers. She had the additional responsibility of maintaining a reputable, pleasant, and economically efficient household; of checking unruly boarders, perhaps, and of chivvying laggard ones.

Her role had aspects of the motherly, wifely, and sisterly to it, as well as involving more business-like management and supervisory skills.

What I know of Ellen's boardinghouse, I learned much later from my mother, who lived there when she was a child, in the early 1930s, by which time her grandmother had been running boardinghouses in different midtown locations for Irish lads for twenty five years or so. One of Ma's jobs was to wake the boarders (for work on weekdays and for Mass on Sundays). Another was to help write letters home for those unable to write for themselves. They'd tell her what to put and she, in her American girl's copperplate, would write it out for them.

I imagine those letters in my mother's hand slipping across the Atlantic, their neatness and prettiness belying the lives they rightly belonged to, that had jags of hardship and loneliness in them, needing to be written smooth.

And you, Ellen, I write into boardinghouse capability, with the confidence of a woman who's learned the run of things; who has, somehow, managed it, this progress—from one daughter among many daughters, to mistress of her own home.

From Glenavoo to square footage in Manhattan, your own name on the lease.

Let no one ever say you've not made something of yourself.

"When it came to furnishings, I took out the only loan I've had.
Maggie gave me lace curtains; Kate crocheted two bedspreads
and I bought the crockery, pans, and flatware at a parish sale.
I don't think I could have done it cheaper, and when it was all
shipshape, the dining table set mannerly, a lamp on the bureau
and the third-hand Brussels carpet scoured clean with ammonia,
it looked good, I don't mind saying, the way any home should,
for Jimmy, Annie, and I to share together, and for good.

"I opened accounts with the butcher and grocer, the lumber
and coal merchants, and got all stocked up. Days, the terror
of the enterprise (and especially the bills) fair gave me pause
but, already, it was too late for any breed of second thoughts.
I was in it up to my neck, committed for better or worse.
If it failed, it was me who'd fail. My name on the lease.

"Irish lads seemed most familiar to me so I stuck with them;
  from the west, if possible, for the accents close to home.
  No Drinking, No Swearing, and No Cards were the rules,
  prompt down at the bell-ring. No politics at meals.
  Rent was due the first of each month, to be paid in full.
  Up and out for Mass on Sundays, unless you were ill.
  No shenanigans in the parlor. If I heard a girl's voice
  where no girl ought to be, it was Pack Your Bags at once.

"But I never had trouble more than the odd snorer in bed
  or that smelly lad from Dromad the others couldn't abide.
  John Byrne broke his ankle at work and was laid up for weeks
  but they paid his rent for him while he read a library of books.
  I never had a boarder I'd not have left alone with Annie,
  and if there were some I didn't much like, it wasn't many."

"If ever I thought running my own house would be softer than service,
I was soon disabused, boarders not being slow to whinge and grouse:
the bedsprings were lax, the mutton was tough, they were sick of hominy
and flounder, they wanted steak and pineapple, oysters, pickled ham.
Food from Astor House, I ask you, for their two dollars fifty a week!
I did my level best, made good pies, hearty soup, and oatmeal, cake
always for a birthday, goose for Christmas, chops on Saint Patrick's Day.
But after food and laundry, there wasn't enough for a maid's pay.

"So, I did it all myself: the cooking, cleaning, wash-up, marketing,
bill-paying, even emptying chamber pots and slop jars, everything
bar laundry: I drew the line at that; sent out weekly to Mrs. Duff
(who'd bleach and iron the wind if it would stand still long enough).
I kept a clean house always, if it killed me. And a fire in the parlor
to welcome them like they were home, which they mostly were."

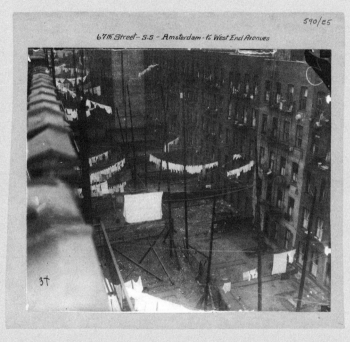

Yards of West 67th Street in 1918, where Ellen is recorded in the 1910 census, with three male boarders with Irish names. Image courtesy of Irma and Paul Milstein Division of United States History, Local History, and Genealogy, New York Public Library.

A veteran landlady interviewed by the New York Times in November 1889 pronounced boardinghouse keeping as "the most cruel and thankless way a woman can earn her living." She ticked off a laundry list of grievances: "weary days and sleepless, anxious nights," suspicious landlords, boarders who treated her "as if she were a sort of an upper servant." Her advice to prospective boardinghouse keepers? "Don't do it."

—QUOTED IN GAMBER (2007, 60)

"You'd live in fear that a lodger would flit in the night
with his rent unpaid, leaving his empty trunk behind
to steal a little time. It never actually happened to me,
I suppose I knew the lads and they were decent sorts,
as a rule, not much older than my Jimmy, plenty keen
to live where linen wasn't changed one sheet a week,
regardless, or unwashed towels moved room to room,
where mattresses had springs, not pigs' hair, unlike some.

"I was fair to them and they to me. If they were ever sick
I'd tend to them and, in their turn, they'd carry a bucket
upstairs for me if they saw me laboring. If they were dirty
in their habits when they came, I'd try to teach them city
ways, not to leave boots in the washbasin or food for rats.
That in New York we say, 'Yes, sir,' and start from scratch."

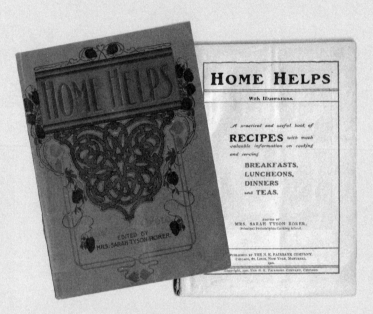

Home Helps: A Practical and Useful Book of Recipes (Chicago: N. K. Fairbank, 1900).

"I had a good array over the years, bartenders and porters,
   locomotive firemen, laborers, salesmen, even a chauffeur!
   If one was leaving to marry or to live closer to a new job
   he'd often find me a replacement and show him the ropes
   so I rarely had to advertise or take a chance on a stranger.
   William Tarpey went to expense and trouble to arrange
   for his brother to join him here, but the lad never showed.
   Despite ads in newspapers, I believe he was never found.

"That happened. We usually tried to look out for our own
   but we weren't always able. Some people want to be alone.
   I never did, preferring voices to none, news of the world
   brought back of an evening to just me rattling round
   an empty flat, no one to jolly me or call me 'Missus,'
   no company but the coal fire or a sometime ghost."

"I often wished my mother could see me, in clothes
  of my own choosing, keeping a respectable house,
  everyone treated civilly, decent room and board
  (if not luxury, exactly, no one went hungry or cold):
  keeping spending tallies every night in the big book,
  settling the merchants' bills, and paying off the bank;
  dishing out supper at six o'clock, the same for each,
  (for fear they'd be practicing their 'boarders' reach').

"I used to think of her dishing up meals for my children,
  seeing their faces turned up to hers. Me at my table
  made up of, if not entire strangers, then not kin;
  her sitting down to eat with them, and me not able.
  Oh, that boardinghouse was a well-made plan
  to get them back, my lost daughter, my lost son."

EIGHT

Returning II

It is time.

Jimmy (aged almost fifteen) and Annie (almost fourteen) have
left their grandparents' home in Glenavoo to sail back to New
York in September 1913. They are returning (though it won't feel
like it) to their mother, Ellen, who can finally offer them a home.
They have Irish accents, perhaps even some Irish (which Anne
and Austin, their grandparents, both spoke, according to census
returns), and only Irish friends. I'm guessing (but I could be
wrong) they've had no contact with their father since they were
both babies (elsewise, how could Ellen have got away with saying
he had died?). With Ellen, I assume their contact to have been
letters, maybe the occasional photograph. For them, Mother is
envelopes coming up the lane, news of people they don't remember or have never met. Everything they know of the world, they
will have learned in Glenavoo.

Now they are sailing to the mother who has sent for them. Are
they fearful, lonely, homesick for their grandparents? I wonder if
maybe Jimmy is excited, being the older of the two. I imagine he
is minding his sister on the journey. She is wide-eyed on the ship,
the harbinger of the twelve-year-old girl, my mother, who will
sail on the *Scythia* in the opposite direction, twenty-three years
on from this.

Austin and Anne wake to rooms emptied of them, as their
daughter has done for the past twelve years. (This is not difficult
for me to imagine, I who have—like so many mothers—come
back from early morning airport runs to lie on my children's

empty beds, and believe I can smell them home.) Anne will be either good for nothing that day, or else in a fury about the house, cleaning what doesn't need to be cleaned, getting head-long through the hours until the cat rubs up against her legs, and something about the softness of it, the way Annie loved that silly tabby, will have her come undone like a row of knitting with an unforgiveable fault. Austin will be busy out in the fields, doing hard work, fencing or clearing a ditch, working until his bones ache with a manageable pain.

It is today. Ellen dresses in her best clothes to go to Ellis Island to meet them off the ship. She stands in the hallway on her way out, throws an eye over the wooden floor she has polished this morning, herself. Thinks of the bedrooms she has readied for them, the beds turned down and neat as pins, the two chairs she had painted bright red to make the rooms look young.

There's a loaf of brown bread cooling beside the stove, the same bread her mother taught her to bake, so they will feel at home.

She steps out into the clear air of the future she's been waiting for, day in, day out these past twelve years, since she left them in Glenavoo.

Is it for me to imagine what happens when they meet?

If there are limits to what I can claim of your life for my purposes, this would seem to ask for them, this reunion.

I will see you again afterward, when you're all three on dry land again, out of the subway car, up the Columbus Circle steps, the two of them stiff as mannequins, not knowing where to look.

Do you watch them scale themselves against a city even taller than it was when you came, over thirty years ago?

The last time the three of you were together here, they were small children; you could hold them both in your arms at the same time, if you needed to.

Now you have to look up to Jimmy, he's inches taller than you. Annie is smaller, so when you stand between them (when they'll let you), it's as if someone has drawn a line from the top of the buildings down to Jimmy's head, over yours and down to hers.

At a church fair at Saint Vincent Ferrer's, I find this stereoscope of the lake at Central Park. If I had the right viewing device, I could see it as a three-dimensional image, combining the views of the right and the left eye.

And if I had the right device to combine what I can see with what I want to see, I could maybe catch the three of you there, walking together as you show them the city, your city, and they tell all you about the home that was your home once, that they've had to leave, just as you had to do.

"The Lake, Central Park," stereoscope by L. G. Strand, Worcester, Massachusetts, ca. 1900.

I HOPE THEY WERE ABLE TO MAKE A HOME in each other, the three of them.

Of course, it wasn't just the three of them: there were Ellen's sisters too, aunts who'd grown up in Glenavoo—able, perhaps, to swoop down on Jimmy and Annie as versions of Anne and Austin.

I'll venture, between them, they talked up the farm, building— ditch by field, gable by cobblestone—a Glenavoo in Manhattan. I hope one of the girls was a good mimic, able to bring a neighbor to life to sit with them at table. Able to catch the inflection or phrase that would lift a person from memory so you could almost picture them walking in, in their unsuitable clothes and rusty habits, any minute.

I wonder about the voices round Ellen's table, how long the Irish accents persisted, how soon they slipped into American, like tributaries into the river. Like children making tents out of sheets and blankets on upturned chairs, did they make with their voices around the table, sentence by sentence, word by word, some kind of home?

Did it work, I wonder? Did they get past being strange to each other, past all the wrong turns and necessary shifts (with their sly compromises and attendant losses) they'd had to undertake? Did they come to love each other, to get on?

There are some questions not even I would put to even a ghost.

Though I look for answers all the same, hearing them in so slight as a chair creak, so much as a whir of words in my own head.

"Jimmy came back restless and fidgety; Annie was quieter.
I felt I was a stranger to them, despite the years of letters.
It was Sally they were closest to from living on the farm,
Sally who was hugged to death. Sally who knew the name
of the dog and the calf at home. Sally who swore blind
they'd love it here once they settled in and made friends,
so certain, even I believed her, or wanted to. I won't deny
it hurt, though, after all my years of plans and putting by.

"They got good at helping me run the boardinghouse.
I gave them jobs: Annie's was to wake the lads for Mass,
Jimmy's to fix any lever, chain, or cog that broke.
Dada taught him. Annie baked what Mama baked,
though it wasn't the same, she said. Thinner. Airy.
I said she'd get used to it, as I had. She said, 'Maybe.'"

I WANT TO GIVE YOU SILK, because there are many pleasures you may never have money nor curiosity nor appetite for, but this is a simple one, a plausible one, easily given to you.

Jimmy buys it for your birthday the first year he is back there with you. He has been working Saturdays in the local garage, learning about engines, coming home to your clucks and eye rolls, covered in grease and oil you can never get to lift clear of his clothes. But you don't mind. He's busy and Mr. Dwyer likes him and says he is quick to learn. You tell Jimmy he's just like his father, head forever stuck under the hood of some engine or other, and it is a pleasant fib, barely even a fib, since his father was a motorman. And there is so little you can tell Jimmy about his father that will not make him think less of himself and his own blood, you're glad of this handy line.

So he works Saturdays and saves up his dollars and when he thinks he has enough, he brings Annie to Lord & Taylor on Fifth Avenue to help him choose. He will say it is from them both, of course, and having Annie with him when he buys it means it's almost true.

He's a good lad, Jimmy. It is going to be his mother's birthday, his mother who has brought him home, as she calls it, and though the word sticks in his throat like his accent did when he came first, he sees that she wants to be motherly, and so decides he will be a son, an attentive son, who knows the right thing to do and can do it, and has money to pay for it too.

Annie hasn't been in Lord & Taylor before now. She stands inside the door as though she's afraid if she takes one more step, it will break the magic spell. Jewelry, gloves, hats, and scent, all of it guarded by shopgirls with elaborate hairdos and pearl necklaces and smiles. Jimmy is glad he has brought Annie, else he wouldn't know where to look.

"A scarf," he says, "a woman's scarf," and one of them points him the way.

"Certainly," the girl at the counter says. "What color would you like?"

Jimmy doesn't know what color he would like and neither does Annie so the shopgirl, who is shiny and pretty, he thinks, lifts up a series of folded squares, shakes them out in front of her, and sets them down on the glass counter for Jimmy to choose from.

For a second, he thinks he is looking at sunlight on a spill of oil on the workshop floor.

And then he thinks he has never seen so many giddy colors in his life.

Annie runs her hands along the top of them and picks out one in green and blue, with a border of orange and gold. "It was the softest," she'll say on the way home, when he asks her why she picked that one. The bloody dearest too, he'll think, but he doesn't want to spoil anything about the box in her hand with the purple ribbon, the scarf inside like a summer day out on the boat on Lough Talt, nothing but blue sky above them and green fields all around, beaded with yellow gorse.

Even he can see the scarf is beautiful and he's glad it was expensive, because he knows his mother will wear it to show the world he loves her, and he will look at her wearing it and see in it a proof of the same thing.

SCARVES WITH A SHIMMER OF LOUGH TALT. Birthday presents and affection. Outings to department stores.

Fancy, every word of it.

I could just stick to the facts.

Which facts?

The facts of the record, of course, in which this family is pinned together in the 1915 New York State census, Ellen, aged forty (she was fifty-three!), James, aged sixteen (office boy), and Annie aged fifteen (still at school), along with boarders Bernard O'Brien (porter) and William Tarpey (locomotive fireman). The "O" before Ellen's surname seems to have been added in after the initial entry for Ellen Grady. It's the first official inclusion of that "O," afterward sanctioned in its proper place in the 1920 census.

In 1920, Annie (aged twenty), still living with her mother, is an accounts clerk.

Jimmy is no longer listed with his mother and sister: presumably he lives elsewhere.

And there we have it, the whole of the facts: name, address, age, and occupation. Nothing else needed now.

But I am no statistician, no historian. I seek other ways to tell the story. Wanting to fill in in those stark, impersonal outlines, I cast around with my poet's eye for color and detail; for something more than a rail of fact to hang the story on.

"When I first set up, I made a pair of yellow velvet drapes
from old fabric a traveling merchant let me have cheap.
They were all the color I never wore and all the luxury
I didn't need, not just how they knew to flip a winter day
to gold, but because they were beautiful, soft to my touch
when everything else I put a hand to was work to be done.
Every apartment I lived in, they were my own, private sun.
Money in, money out. But those drapes made me feel rich.

"No matter if the day collapsed, something got solved at night
by pulling those gold curtains on its lack. That's how I lived.
shutting the world and all its claims and tiredness and debt
beyond the window, keeping safe and small as I could within.
That's how it was in Glenavoo, if without a drape in sight,
our evening stories pushing back the brutal dark outside."

AND OPENED THEM, THOSE DRAPES, every school morning, hooshing the children out the door.

. . . And closed them every evening on heads bent over books.

(You and your talk about schooling and the good of it. You'd tell them both about how the lack of it would be a stone tied to their ankles; told them over dinner about Mr. Ford in Glenavoo, how if you hadn't a penny to put in his jar, he'd turn you back out the door. Not that the penny got you very far, unless it was poetry you were after, all of you in unison bleating out "I remember, I remember the house where I was born" or "A Nation Once Again" to the sound of his hand beating down on his desk like a hammer on a nail in a plank. But you did learn how to read and write and tally numbers, and where would you have been without that, trying to run a boardinghouse and keep the ledger shipshape? So, up with them every morning and out with a good meal inside them, your own eye fixed [if theirs was not] on a future softer than any version of one you'd been able to permit yourself.

Jimmy wasn't one for book learning, but Annie kept her head down. "It's no load to carry," you'd say and you said it so often, she used to tease you whenever she came upon you carrying a tub of laundry or a bag of groceries. "Is that a load to carry, then?" she'd ask, skipping right by you.)

. . . And opened them, those velvet drapes, on the morning, one week shy of his twentieth birthday, when Jimmy was drafted in the third U.S. Army registration, on September 12, 1917.

U.S. Army registration card for James O'Grady. Records of the Selective Service System (World War I), 1917–1919, U.S. National Archives microfilm publication, M1509.

. . . AND OPENED THEM, THOSE VELVET DRAPES, the morning he came home.

. . . And opened them the morning Annie walked out to her first job, as a stenographer, delighted with herself and you with her too, who would never be a servant now and would always have a skill to fall back on.

. . . And opened them every morning of her young womanhood, the life you didn't have, that you loved in her.

. . . And on the day after she met Thomas O'Boyle.

. . . And on the morning in June 1923, when she married him.

. . . And on the morning of June 10, 1924, when their daughter, my mother, Ellen Bridget O'Boyle, came into this world.

It's a waltham ladies pocket watch, of a kind popular in the early 1920s. Gold with a cream face and black hands and numerals. Tiny slips of sapphire at the tips of both the hands.

Of course, it doesn't work.

My mother gave it to me; it had been given to her as a christening gift. By whom—her parents? Possible, but unlikely. It was 1924. I don't suppose there was a lot of spare cash for gold watches knocking round.

Tommy's parents were back in Mayo: I doubt gold watches for American babies were a priority.

So, I write it as your gift, Ellen, to your first grandchild who has been named for you, a gold watch from a grandmother who no longer needs to save every penny to rescue other people's lives.

If I'm right (and who will say I am not?), this watch will have passed through your hands. It might even have been set, one time, by you.

When I was a student in Dublin, I used to pass the second-floor workshop of an ancient watchmaker overlooking College Green at the gates of Trinity College. Unbeknownst to my mother, I took the watch and brought it to him to fix as a surprise for her, a way to give her back something of the stories she'd given me.

But there was no fixing it.

If you know the trick of it, you can raise the catch at the top of the watch so the back springs open to expose the mechanism. Wheels and cogs and tiny screws. A serial number. Some patterning around the edge of the steel. It's a beautiful piece of engineering, even if it doesn't do what it was intended to do.

All its separate parts, dainty and tight and interlocking: more purpose to them than the telling of time, or even the telling of several times, each one true in its way.

NINE

Not My Ellen

ELLEN: SHAPESHIFTER; flitting ghostly through the record, leaving the lightest trace.

- Ellen O'Hara (baptism record, 1862)
- Ellen G. Hara (marriage certificate, 1898)
- Ellinor Grady (1900 census)
- Ellen Gready (*Umbria* passenger manifest, 1901)
- Ellen Grady (1910 census)
- Ellen OGrady (1915 census)
- Ellen O'Grady (1920 census)
- Ellen O'Grady (1925 census)
- Ellen O'Grady (1930 census)
- Ellen O'Grady (death certificate, 1950)

My eyes are sore from riffling through screen after screen of census records (I've been doing it for days), every one of them promising solution and certainty, until I click on it and it does not.

I feel like Gerard Manley Hopkins, close to death, complaining he was afflicted by rheumatism of the eyes.

I want to claim it too: I am afflicted by rheumatism of the eyes. When I drag my glance across the screen, I can practically hear them creak. I am equally afflicted by rheumatism of the past, how stiff and unwieldy and boring it is, when it won't move as we'd like it to, when it won't keep up with us.

I fancy Ellen with a stubborn streak, and a wicked laugh. I feel entitled to. I'm sure she must be laughing at me, rummaging and rummaging in a past, so many pasts, having nothing whatsoever to do with hers.

It's not nothing to conjure you out of thin air and have you sit in judgment in my office, finding me wanting, as you do. It's a curious, self-punishing, thankless, coiled affair.

Sometimes I lose track of if I'm me or you; if the world at my window is now or then; wonder if, when I leave, you might remain; whether you sound far too much like I do.

Sometimes, I want to tell you about my life, my children, what I'm doing with all this, the point of so much examining your life.

Sometimes I imagine I'm not here either, or here only the same way that you are: as words through which both of us pass.

Today, you look tired. Those circles under your eyes
at first I took for the shadow of your hat, are lines
the same shade of winter as those on my own face.
I get a cushion, arrange the air around you like a vase
of gladioli or calla lilies, significant and deathly white,
while you, as if on a dimmer you alone can operate,
come as you please, fade out and in, tarry or flit
depending on how you choose to work the light.

"Don't go," I say. "You don't need to say anything
but keep me company. Please do." And there it is.
I'm begging a ghost to mind me from the shadows
lengthening under me now, for fear I would fall in.
And she does. We sit in silence, our eyes closed
until evening shuts the day's white, winter rose.

Samhain. all souls' night. halloween. The veil separating this world and the next is at its thinnest, so the dead can return. In your Ireland, you would have set an extra place at table and put a bowl of water there, unlatched the door and lit a candle for every dead soul of close kin. All to make them welcome, should they return to sit a while.

I have left a sliced apple on a saucer for you. I feel foolish so I bin it once it browns.

We are not usual, you and me, or this way of doing things.

My screen is a veil through which you pass with your umbrella, or you don't. I can't invite you, I can't refuse you. But when you stay away, it's as if the way I think of your life is solid and dark, like being in a warehouse full to the ceiling with identical black boxes. This fact and that fact. This trend, that data set. There is no give, no subtlety.

And when I have you sit opposite me over there, all the reading I do of studies and reports—it's as if lit from the inside by a small, persistent glow.

"Are you not sick of it yet?" she asks. "Why don't you
  just accept there are some things you'll never know?"
"Such as?" A trick question asked by an adult of a child,
  but I'm getting desperate for details. And I'm tired.
"Bored?" She leans in. "I'd say it's time to give up, maybe.
  For all your looking, you might find we were ordinary,
  all of us as scant and laggard with answers as I am.
  What you discover in the end could be a waste of time."

Of course, I can't do it. I want to fill in every gap,
  record by record, fact by fact, clue by telling clue
  until every crucial detail in this narrative lines up
  and I have solved your life, somehow restoring you.

As if. What am I playing at? "Good question, that!"
  she says. "A great shame it lacks an answer, isn't it?"

SOMETIMES I FEEL AS THOUGH genealogical research is like walking through a corridor I've never been in before, with thousands of differently colored streamers hanging down. Fifteen of them, scattered in among the others, are red and my task is to find them. But the corridor is dark and I am blindfolded. The streamers brush against my face. I would like to use my hands to clear a passage for walking through, but I cannot, because someone has tied them behind me with a streamer I see as red, though, of course, it might not be.

Fifteen Streamers: Not My Ellen

1. The *New York Times* of May 29, 1888, reports that "twenty six English sovereigns, $20 in bills and other small amounts in silver and pennies were found concealed on the person of Ellen O'Hara who died in the Albany Almshouse today. She came to this country from Ireland about two years ago."

2. From the *Cincinnati Enquirer*, January 20, 1897: "Senator Bryce's Bill granting a pension of $3 per month to Ellen O'Hara was favorably reported in the Senate today."

3. In 1900, Ellen O'Grady is living in Manhattan. Born in New York in November 1872 to a father born in Massachusetts and a mother in England, this Ellen is not laundress, dressmaker, or servant. This Ellen, who is single, is a teacher in the establishment of Margaret Cullen at 328 Broadway.

4. From the *Philadelphia Inquirer*, April 12, 1901:

    GRADY, *On April 8, 1901, Mrs. Ellen Grady, widow of the late John Grady, funeral on Friday morning at 8 o'clock from Northwest corner Thirty-fifth and Sunnyside Avenue, Falls of Schuylkill. High requiem mass at St. Brigid's church. The League of the Sacred Heart and the Altar Society of St Brigid's Church invited. Interment at St Charles Cemetery, Kellyville.*

5. In Lima, Ohio, the *Cincinnati Enquirer* of August 6, 1904, reports that "Mrs. Albert Driver (aged 50) is dying and Mrs. Ellen Grady (aged 60) is in a serious condition as the result of a runaway accident, their horse having become frightened at a passing train."

6. In Pittsburgh, the *Gazette Times* of July 6, 1913, reports that Mrs. Ellen Grady was in attendance at the St Paul's Orphan Asylum annual Orphans Picnic, seated at the "Epiphany" table, alongside Miss L. Blanchard and Mrs. J. O'Brien.

7. The *New York Times* of January 2, 1918, reports that "Mrs. Ellen O'Grady, widow, 67 years old who lived on Old House Landing Road in Little Neck, Long Island, died there yesterday from burns she received late Monday night when her clothing was ignited while she was lighting an oil stove."

8. Ellen O'Grady, born in Ireland in 1873, came to the United States in 1889. In 1910, she's living on Richardson Street in Brooklyn with her husband, John, a driver with the Express Company. She has given birth to fourteen children, of whom seven live. (By the census of 1915, two more of those—Mary and Julia—have also died.)

9. On February 8, 1920, the *New York Herald Tribune* reports that "many society women will be patronesses of the charity ball to be given by the Knights of Columbus at the Hotel Astor on the evening of February 14th. Cooperating with the women's auxiliary which is engaged in preparations for the Ball are: Miss Elsa Maxwell, Mrs. Ellen O'Grady and Mrs. Frederic Neilson."

10. On January 7, 1915, the *Toronto Globe* reports that an electrical explosion in a conduit between the Fiftieth and Fifty-Ninth Street stations brought the New York subway to a halt. "New York's subway was visited by fire and panic today, which landed some 200 persons in hospitals, caused the death of one woman, and demoralized the transportation system of the city. The person killed was Miss Ellen Grady, a stenographer."

11. On August 19, 1928, the *Daily Boston Globe*, under the heading "Real Estate Transactions," reports that "a six-room frame house, sun parlor, modern improvements, 110 Lovell Road, Watertown, has been sold through the concern to Ellen Grady for a home."

12. This may well be the same Ellen Grady who, on January 3, 1929, is reported in the *Daily Boston Globe* to be suing Andrew Amadel for $1000 for personal injuries sustained while riding in his automobile in Newburyport on September 5, 1927.

"Subway Fire," Bain News Service photograph, January 7, 1915. Image courtesy of the Library of Congress, Prints and Photographs Division, Washington, DC. *http://hdl.loc. gov/loc.pnp/ggbain.18110.*

Mrs. Ellen O'Grady, deputy police commissioner of the NYPD, 1918. Photo courtesy of the Bain Collection, Library of Congress, Prints and Photographs Division, Washington, DC. *http://hdl.loc.gov/loc.pnp/ggbain.26059.*

13. In 1920, Ellen Grady lives with her younger sister, Kate, on Edgecombe
    Avenue. She is single and works from home as a dressmaker. In 1930,
    the two sisters have moved to West 169th St, where they are still
    dressmaking. In the same building lives Bertha M. Hoyt (fifty-five), a
    German-born widow who lists her occupation as "actress." By 1935
    (Kate presumably having died), Bertha and Ellen are sharing a home,
    as they still are in 1940, when Bertha is listed as Ellen's "partner."

14. On January 29, 1918, Ellen O. O'Grady, a Brooklyn widow with three
    daughters, became the fifth (and first woman) deputy police commis-
    sioner of the New York City Police Department (NYPD).

    Seldom out of the news, Mrs. O'Grady's more conspicuous campaigns
    included her April 1919 drive against immorality in the motion pictures.
    According to the *New York Times* of April 10, she had spent the previ-
    ous day "going from one movie show to another, mostly in the poorer
    districts of the city," concluding that "the clergy, educators, judges
    and welfare workers of all sorts might as well lock up the churches,
    shut the books, close the courts, if they are going to permit the filthy
    motion pictures being shown in New York . . . to continue."

    That same year, she also supported Mrs. Griswold Wentz's campaign
    against the exhibition of "immodest lingerie" in store windows across
    New York's shopping districts. (Mrs. Wentz also objected, she told
    the *New York Times* of February 27, to the latest style of French gowns,
    which had "no sleeves . . . or only a little satin band"—for a bodice—
    and called for the use of more material in the design of evening gowns.)

    In May, officers acting on Mrs. O'Grady's instructions carried out
    a raid on the headquarters of "Oom the Omnipotent," a.k.a. Pierre
    Bernard. Mr. Bernard was not, however at the scene: according to the
    New York Tribune of May 2, he was discovered to be in attendance at a
    session of the "Crystal Gazers," at which, for a fee of $50, he promised
    to grant relatives a view of their menfolk engaged in action on the
    battlefields of France, and assurances of their safe return.

In June, Mrs. O'Grady visited the courthouse pen of Gordon Fawcett Hamby, lately convicted of a double murder during a $13,000 robbery at the East Brooklyn Savings Bank, and sentenced to die by electric chair in July 1919. . . . Hamby told the *New York Tribune* on June 27, "She is a very nice lady. She nearly made me cry. I just can't stand women when they begin to talk about home and family."

In November, Mrs. O'Grady oversaw the raiding of the offices of a New York matrimonial bureau that promised that anyone placing an ad for $25 could be assured of securing a millionaire wife.

Mrs. O'Grady resigned in 1920, citing interference in her work from within the NYPD.

15. In 1910, Ellen O'Grady, fifty-six, who came to the United States in 1869, is an inmate of the Manhattan State Hospital for the Insane.

ALL THESE ELLENS SURFACE in the course of my research. The New York Public Library has the assembled knowledge, you'd think, of so much of the world in stacks connected, someway, to my room, my chair, your chair, the line between them.

And yet the holes in all this knowledge are deep and dark, like looking up at the space between stars on a winter's night.

Ellen, my starry ancestor.

Ellen, my unknowable, unknown.

If the dead really could talk to us, what do you think they would say? (The unsayable, for instance, that they have knowledge of and we don't, not yet?)

Or would they talk about this and that, who has their engagement ring now, or if so-and-so ever paid the money they owed them, or if the title deeds ever showed up?

I require Ellen to give me (whether or not she is so inclined) information. Proof.

And she, I suppose, might consider the fact of me likewise.

Ellen from Glenavoo, Glen of Ghosts, who would you have called upon, if you'd felt the need?

What ghosts did you carry here in your carpetbag and in your dreams, and in your heart of hearts?

I ask this in the silence of my office, when I've switched off the computer and the lamps, and the day is done. All the records and databases are powered down, the tabs all exited, and the books all closed.

There is the fact of me in my black chair, and the notion of you in the corner, sitting on the wooden one.

I think maybe you have imagined me. Of course you did. And every mother after you in my family line. I was conjured into being by women whose bodies stated an extraordinary (but also a simple) fact, as mine did with my own son and daughter.

Oh, Ellen, with your doughty shadow, your voice thrown into mine, what became of you and your world?

Where did everyone go?

In darkness, my hand pulls the office door to. I step out into a city of ghosts, bringing my own ghosts and your own ghosts with me.

TEN

Loose Change

ELLEN'S LIFE WAS HER OWN, of course, though I'm laying claim to it: to her decisions, her facts, her ins and outs, to the sway of her biography.

Which can only ever be partial, since she has left no trace I know of but bloodline.

But Ellen's life glanced against other lives. The facts as I know them are not unusual (except, perhaps, for leaving her children in Glenavoo). Her husband's desertion, her transplanted sisters and her boardinghouse—these I find in other accounts. These seem typical.

From her life I conjecture parallel lives, a whole way of going on.

From her, I extrapolate, I generalize. I hear in how I make coins rattle in her purse a chime with so many other purses, so many other ways of being real.

All these Irish women working, as Ellen did, in service. And later, grappling up some flimsy social ladder to keep house for themselves. Never, I'll hazard, flush with money. Never, I daresay, having more than was needed any given day. And yet they sent home (by the millions) what they had sore need of in America.

As you'll have done.

What became of it, all this putting by and minding pennies and depositing them in savings accounts where the bank teller got to know you by name and didn't mock the coins you turned out on the counter, tallied perfectly?

You sent them back to where you'd come from, their passage an opposite version of yours, everything about your leaving flipped, by dint of a well-packed envelope, to relief; to joy.

Sent how?

By cash, sometimes via the parish priest (less likely to be stolen). By money order drawn on the Emigrant Industrial Savings Bank. By the Western Union Company (which began an international money transfer service in 1871). By prepaid passage on transatlantic ships (which could be cashed in, for a change of mind).

And if every sum of money sent back had a note, the sound of them crossing back the Atlantic would have had the heft of symphonies.

Money arriving in Glenavoo must have seemed like some magic trick: it began with an extra daughter's body and ended with that body vamoosed, replaced by rent money, settled bills, animals bought in, and the hay to feed them. Another year secured.

Resolving to do something to better the circumstances of her family, the young Irish girl leaves her home for America . . . From the first moment, she saves every cent she earns . . . To keep her place, or retain her employment, what will she not endure?—sneers at her nationality, mockery of her peculiarities, even ridicule of her faith, though the hot blood flushes her cheek with fierce indignation. At every hazard the place must be kept, the money earned, the deposit in the savings-bank increased.

—JOHN FRANCIS MAGUIRE ([1868] 1969, 319)

Irish domestic servants seem to be the most successful and save more money than any class of working girls, as they are at little or no expence.

—PATRICK MCKEOWN, LETTER TO HIS SISTERS IN LISBURN, APRL 22, 1894, QUOTED IN MILLER (2008, 319)

Returned emigrants always said it was easier for girls to save money in America than for men. They were not exposed as much to the temptation to drink and gamble as men, and did not go out of doors to the same extent.

—IRISH FOLKLORE COMMISSION, QUOTED IN RHODES (1992, 255–56)

"Money. Money. Is that all you want to talk about,
 as if no other part of my life could mean anything?
 Not the laughing with other girls, not the dancing
 nor walking out, Sunday afternoons, hair pinned up
 like a lady's, me in my good dress, no apron or cap?
 Not the work done, copper pans shining in sunlight,
 a wholesome meal, a blouse laundered crisp white,
 bread from the oven, cooling; a room made right?

"But my hands were good for more than holding dollar bills
 and my legs for more than running up and down stairs
 in someone else's house, at a stranger's beck and call.
 Money I earned and money I sent wasn't my only care.
 My bank account gave scant account of all I could do
 or was good for: what I loved and everything I knew."

Irish Emigrant Society money order for three pounds sterling. Image courtesy of the National Library of Ireland, MS 41, 773.

"I'd often wonder what it would have been like
  to be one of my brothers, better at farm work,
  and all his sisters in America, good as gold,
  sending home the best part of what they earned
  and glad to help, asking nothing in return
  but letters now and then with news of home.
  Would that be easier, to be dependent but safe,
  with that safety resting on my sisters, not myself?

"Or was it better to be just as I was, the daughter
  who did as was required, so every bill or debt
  at home was a problem to be fixed in America?
  That I, without a farthing over there, or job or say,
  should here earn the money the farm would need
  to be safe and sound: was that a sweeter deal?"

"Yes, to start, money was a good enough reason to be here
but a reason falls short of a life. Not long until a life begins
to accrue as a routine: at one stall you buy meat, at another
John from Baal calls you Ellen and remembers all your kin;
there's the route you like to take to church, the walking boots
with your name inked on, lined up beside all the other boots
as if you lived there. Which you do now. Your pew at Mass.
The letters in your father's hand to your New York address.

"Little by little, the money comes to seem not the main thing,
but still you'd always send back something, knowing the way
they'd hope for it, and you'd hate to think of them opening
an empty letter and finding no money order, turning away,
cross and disappointed, from all your carefully written news.
Money was how you made certain they still held you close."

In Boston . . . during the four weeks ending on Dec 20, 1879, drafts to the number of 2,250 and representing 5,376 pounds, passed through (the teller's) hands. The senders were almost exclusively servant girls.
—DONAHOE'S MAGAZINE (MAY 1880), QUOTED IN HOTTEN-SOMERS (2003, 234)

The biggest contribution to the incomes of the families hereabouts comes from America, from sums sent out of earnings made there. With the contribution that almost every family receives at certain times in the year, each household contrives to pay its shop debts and buy the year's stock—a few sheep and perhaps, a calf.
—PADRAIC COLUM (1926, 167)

"Dada was good about writing back how the money was spent—
sometimes on an animal or on seed, but mostly it was for rent.
I used to like to picture Mama buying a new dress or a nice hat,
something pleasant for herself, but I doubt she was let near it
for the likes of such frippery. It was safety against hard times,
as Dada used say of it: money to keep the wolf from the door,
and the roof over their heads, who lived in every kind of fear
of being turned out for no good reason, on the agent's whim.

"How could you begrudge it to them, when it was put like that?
As years went by, I used to wonder if they had need of it quite
the same way anymore, with two of us sending, then three,
four and five envelopes, monthly, of our hard-earned money
going to Aclare. And us five delighted with ourselves, to think
of the big hand we were giving them, our money in their bank."

In DECEMBER 1863, Austin O'Hara had signed a lease to rent from Samuel Robinson a property at Glenavoo, at the yearly rent of £6-13-6, payable half-yearly. The lease was to run for thirty-one years or for the natural life of Austin, "whichever should longest continue."

Low rent: the land must have been bad. The Griffith's Valuation map put the holding right beside Lough Talt, so it may have been prone to flooding, or was little better than marshland.

Either way, the rent had to be paid.

In 1890, when Ellen was working as a domestic servant and, presumably, sending money back to her parents via remittances, £6-13-6 was equivalent to approximately $34.* Based on Lucy Salman's research findings about average wages for servants in 1889, this represented approximately ten weeks' wages.[†]

Ellen could hardly have been expected to solely bankroll the annual rent, except in times of emergency, perhaps, if the harvest had failed entirely. Nor can she have been expected, surely, to hand over 100 percent of her earnings. In addition, there would have been other claims on whatever money she did remit (bodies, even maidservants', having requirements of their own).

Without records of her financial goings-on, I can't say for certain how much Ellen earned, saved, spent, or remitted home. But I'd hazard a guess this last was not an insignificant amount, as her work as a live-in servant did not require her to spend much in the way of weekly necessities. She may not have earned a fortune (mill girls and even waitresses earned more), but what she earned was, to a fair extent, disposable income to be distributed as she saw fit, at least until she married, which we know she didn't do until in her early thirties, when she'd already been working in New York for about fifteen years.

....

* Doan (1999, 282).

[†] Salmon found the average weekly wage for female domestics in the eastern United States to be $3.60, considerably more than in the South ($2.22), but less than along the less populated Pacific Coast ($4.57). The overall U.S. weekly average was $3.23. Salmon (1897, 88).

THE 1901 IRISH CENSUS B1 FORM returns the O'Hara homestead at Glenavoo as a Class 3 house (meaning it had three, four, or five rooms, with two windows to the front). By 1911, the next census, an extra room has been added: there are now three windows to the front of the house, and it has been raised to a Class 2 house, (meaning it has five or six rooms).

In 1911, as in 1901, Austin's home has four outbuildings, a cow house, a piggery, a fowl house, and a barn. Almost every house in the townland has a cow house (thirty-nine out of forty homes), and most have a piggery (twenty-three), but fowl houses and barns are more rare (only eight of each). In fact, Austin's is one of the better-equipped homes: only two out of forty have five outbuildings (with an additional shed or calf house); four others have four outbuildings, and the remaining forty-three have three or fewer.

It seems fair to say the O'Haras are holding their own in Glenavoo.

To claim that this has come about independently of the remittances sent home by Ellen and her five sisters would be fanciful. Their money must have secured the improvements their family in Glenavoo can now afford.

There is hardly a family in the West of Ireland that does not receive regular remittances from America, and it is not uncommon to find cases of their being sent, within a year, as much as a hundred dollars from, say, two girls who have found places in New York or Boston.

The following are verified statistics. Every year the Union of Clifden receives, through the Clifden Bank, over £10,000 sterling in money from America, in fact over half the amount due for rents from the 3,300 families in the district; so that throughout the West of Ireland the landlords' rents are often merely a tax levied on the filial piety of child emigrants from the peasant families!

—LOUIS PAUL-DUBOIS (1908, 305)

The aggregate sum of remittances . . . amounted to an annual average return of at least $5,000,000 or a grand total of over $260,000,000 in the period from 1848 to 1900.

—ARNOLD SCHRIER (1958, 105)

THINK OF IT, EVERY ACRE SECURED, every room built on, every
barn put up, every cow bought in, every new pair of sturdy
shoes, every dowry allowed to a younger daughter, every tool and
implement, every stick of furniture, every new roof or window or
pot—all of it bought with dollars earned by Irish men in overalls,
sure, but also by Irish women in aprons minding their manners
in the drawing rooms of New York and Boston and Philadelphia,
helping to raise children not their own or to feed mouths that had
never known hunger, to serve oddly named food on dining tables
no bailiff would ever seize.

Dollar by dollar, pound by pound, these women helped build
Modern Ireland. And because they stayed single longer and
worked (predominantly) in jobs that allowed them to save what
they earned, it seems these women were in a position to send
more money home than their male counterparts did.* And send
they did.

There they are, sealing up notes inside news of each other and
only good things said about their lives, writing names on envelopes,
imagining them opened at the other end, the notes counted, cal-
culations made, Father and Mother sitting down that evening to a
fire they knew would not now be put out by any capricious breeze.

Picture the envelopes of all the Ellens, Bridgets, Maggies, and
Kates landing letter by letter, farm by farm, family by family.

Picture lights in windows across Ireland, winter months. Families inside playing cards, children doing homework or reading
letters out from aunts they maybe don't remember, or maybe
have never met.

Those aunts are names at the end of letters that fade over
years to being only names, rarely called upon, lodged gently in the
gaps of memory, as a bottle might be in a stone wall, to be pulled
out by some future child who will dust it down, hold it up against
the light and love the color coming through.

....
* Diner (1983, 47).

"Well, there we are. We left to live in other people's houses
and to send back only our success and not our loneliness.
We made a country by our swollen hands and aching feet,
by holding our tongues or passing up a new coat or shoes
to fill the next bank order plump. We made a country fit
to live in, though we chose not to, or couldn't. And we put
more than money in those envelopes: in went the best part
of us too; our girlhood. Lightheartedness. Our young days.

"If we'd kept what we sent I wonder where we'd be now:
In houses with our names on deeds, no one to put us out,
our children earning nicely, maybe their own companies,
and their children in no doubt about going to university?
About as far removed from want as New York from Aclare.
Maybe it took longer here because of what we sent back there?"

LATER, WHEN SUCCESSIVE LAND ACTS made it possible for tenant farmers to buy out their leases all over Ireland, did the confidence to borrow the purchase price arise from the remittances sent home by children that allowed for savings accounts?

Austin did not buy out his lease on the farm at Glenavoo. It lapsed when he died in January 1921 and Anne moved to an address at Kilcummin, nine miles away. Maybe they felt too old for fresh starts. Maybe their remaining sons had sights set on better farms elsewhere. Maybe they preferred small rent to large debt.

I'll never know.

But if Austin and Anne chose not to buy their farm, many chose differently.

In the period of two years (1906–1908), nearly 100,000 tenants, close to one fifth of the entire number of farm occupiers in Ireland, became purchasers of their holdings.

—ELIZABETH HOOKER (1938, 82)

By 1913, 67% of all land had been transferred to occupier ownership.

—ROBERT A. DOAN (1999, 387)

When the Free State Treaty was proclaimed in 1922, Ireland had been converted into a country of peasant proprietors. Under the system of direct sales under the Acts of 1903–1909 nearly 200,000 peasants were enabled to become owners of their holdings. Nearly 6,250,000 acres of land passed from landlord to peasant....

In all more than a half of the soil of Ireland had been transferred to the Irish peasants.

—JOHN E. POMFRET (1930, 306)

A MODEST PROPOSAL OF MY OWN:

- ♦ that Ireland's early twentieth-century independence movement was underwritten by the economic confidence of a people now secure in its land ownership;
- ♦ that this security was, in turn, underwritten by remittances sent back home by emigrant sons and daughters (though mainly, if contemporary accounts are to be credited, by daughters);
- ♦ that the link, therefore, between the work of Irish women abroad and the foundation of the Irish state is clear and strong (if largely unacknowledged).

Those nicely plumped-up savings accounts, the bills settled, the farms well stocked and asked to support so many children fewer, the outhouses built, the homes made more cozy and sanitary—is it fanciful to project that pride in one's homestead could feed into national pride?

Is it wishful to believe that the good of the money those daughters scrimped to send home didn't end with those homes, exactly, but fed into a movement that gathered strength over the early part of the twentieth century; that resulted, at last, in an Ireland better fit to live in for those who stayed behind?

"Don't forget us daughters of the house, lost but not lost,
 who pulled you back, time and again, from the lip of harm.
 Don't forget us, who never forgot, but kept you steadfast
 in our heart of hearts, your lost girls who took dark rooms
 and brightened them with kindness and tokens of our love;
 who sent back envelopes, no matter what, year in, year out
 that your homes (our homes), should be tended and safe.
 Don't forget us ever, your lost daughters of the house.

"Grant me this, who once was one of them. Stand beside
 that girl in her stiff new leaving coat, a bag in her hand
 with a future in it packed like the city sky she'll see in days.
 Tell her that her life ahead will lift all she leaves behind,
 that they'll thrive, and their children will, because she goes.
 Maybe the knowing will shorten for her that lonely road."

ELEVEN

Home

MONEY FATED YOU. Money decided you. Money framed your life.

The want of it. The lure of it. And the chance of it.

According to my mother, sometime in spring 1936 her father, Thomas (Thos) O'Boyle, won a pub in Ballyhaunis, Co. Mayo in a New York poker game.

Imagine that game, the moment when the stake is raised, the hand played, the bare-faced truth of the cards on the table, the pub lost. And the pub won. One man undone, one man made up. My grandfather wanting to whoop and whistle and maybe, just maybe, able to hold back. The man opposite him who, a minute ago, had been cocksure of his hand (or else reckless, maybe, giddy and urgent, wanting to throw all he had into the fire of another man's luck and simply start over) not so giddy now. He's wondering, I'm guessing, will my grandfather relent, say the game was no way fair so the stakes are null and void.

My grandfather does not relent. The pub is his now, and home to his wife and children he goes, title deeds in his breast pocket, a future beginning to open before him as the first smear of light behind the skyline, with its brand new day.

(It's a good story, punch-drunk on drama and consequence. Every life should have such a story, I think, with knife-edge tension and a win at the end, not at all the kind of punch line to be grafted neatly onto any of those Biddy jokes.

But one detail bothers me. In poker, everyone bets equally, right? If you can't *see* the stakes, you fold. You're out, you cannot win. So Thos would have had to have something to produce to *see* that pub. Something someway equal, whatever that would have been.

Perhaps he bluffed and got lucky.

Or perhaps he came upon a pub in Ireland by some other, less winning, means. Prohibition had ended in 1933; perhaps there were other ways a man with a bathtub and a recipe had come by the price of a small public house in a small Irish town, and a story to cover his tracks?

No, I'm sticking with the poker game. Who am I to refuse luck?)

What I know for sure is that with the deeds of a pub in his possession, miraculously (no matter how you look at it), Thos decides to take his family home.

No question of allowing Ellie to remain in New York, though she pleads to stay with her granny who also asks, more quietly (with the sound of the *Etruria*'s engines in her head, maybe), if it might be so.

It might not.

Annie is firm. She will not abandon any one of her children. They will return to Ireland as a family.

That goodbye is not for me. I cannot witness my mother's hurt, nor the shadow that parting would throw down on her life.

To witness is to lay a claim—a claim too close to home.

I move on, ahead of trunks and boarding, cabins with their doll's-house sinks and menus that seem the most exciting thing in the world, until they don't anymore. Manhattan shortening as they pull away until they can fit it between fingers and thumb. And then not even that.

ON THE DECK OF THE *SCYTHIA*, my mother is photographed, smiling, in her beret and belted gabardine, in the company of three women in coats with fur collars, none of them Ellen.

Stirred by her misery, these kind, expensive women have decided to chivvy her along. Yes, of course, they will call for her on their way home and take her back to New York. Yes, of course, they will bring her to her grandmother. Yes, of course, that will be fine.

She waited, she told me, by the window, for the car to come up Knox Street, for fur collars to emerge. For those women, her friends, who understood, who had *promised*, to firmly call her away from this family that she hardly knew; from a town of children who laughed at her accent and told her to pick the pretty nettles for her mother and wore old shoes with holes in them and threw dirt at her gabardine; from the strange language she didn't understand; from the cold, even in summer; from the gray, the driving rain.

She waited for weeks and then told herself she'd been stupid, they'd not come. They'd gone back to New York without her and she must live in this new life, and make the best of it.

Ellen never saw Ellie again.

She died on December 4, 1950.

At some point my mother switched from Ellie to Helen, from New York to Ireland, from Ellen to her rightful mother, Anna O'Boyle, wife of Thos, of Knox Street, Ballyhaunis. She went back in 1976, met her Uncle Jimmy, and visited Ellen's grave.

I wonder if she heard, with better right than I, her grandmother's voice talking back to her there, filling in the blank from that morning when Ellie and Annie and Thos and all boarded the *Scythia* in New York, and simply crossed back home.

I sit in my door-closed office, imagining the stories brought over to Ireland on that ship, and the stories left behind. That they'd be sure to see each other soon. That they'd write. That Ellie would come back next summer. That the ocean between them was grooved already with their comings and goings, and no need for an end to that.

Above my computer are shelves of books that have given me an outline. The computer has databases with countless facts to tether this story to some version of reality. My fingers type words that claim to know what it is they might be doing.

So much context; so many boreens into your story that could, all of them, be dead ends.

Your chair in the corner is a lull of shadow and is full of the lack of you.

So I conjure you there again. I have to, to tell the story true, to get to the quick of it.

Your head is bowed, your hands are fallow. And your voice when I finally hear it sounds too much like my own.

"I'm not saying it wasn't lonely after Tommy and Annie sailed,
and that I didn't miss Ellie something sore about the place,
all those questions of hers piled up, no need for answers now
and no need to buy her watermelons or cook her favorite stew.

"Little Ellie. It was a fierce, heavy silence she left here after her.
I think I died of it, that black silence, like a poison in my heart.
I must have sent her a hundred letters, but she sent none back.

"She forgot me, I suppose. Or Ireland was too much of a shock
to find words to describe. The wee girl. I'd have kept her here,
but Annie said she wouldn't do to Ellie what I'd done to her.

"Of course, she didn't need to, with her husband by her side.
Funny, isn't it, the way these things come around and go around.
Jimmy and Annie in Aclare. Annie and Thos in Ballyhaunis.
And Ellen O'Grady, to die in New York. Ellen O'Hara as was."

I KNOW SOMETHING YOU DON'T KNOW. My mother, Helen
O'Boyle, did write back to you, every week for years, religiously.

But you didn't get those letters because they were never
sent. Annie burned them, as she did yours to Helen, because she
thought there was no point in both of you upsetting yourselves.
Out of sight, out of mind. So she burned the letters going each
way and only told Ma about them after you, Ma's granny, died.

You must each have thought the other had forgotten you, but I
know that's not so.

It seems cruel to me, but I don't know what those letters to a
granddaughter meant to the daughter who'd been billetted in Co.
Sligo, by a mother gone back to New York.

What a silence to come between them. What a silence to have
to share.

I WONDER HOW ANNIE ACCOUNTED TO ELLEN for the lack of word from Helen. Or how she squared it with herself, the letter-burning.

Did she understand it as a lashing-out against a mother who had abandoned her, and a daughter who preferred that grand-mother, no two ways about it, to the right mother who had not left her daughter in another country (no matter how much she pleaded for it), but had brought her, kit and caboodle, howling and grieving, all the way to their new family life?

I don't suppose she did, because, surely, if you understood that, you'd stop burning them at some point, to allow those wounds to heal?

Instead, you'd tell yourself you were doing it for your daughter's good, of course you would. Probably my mother kicked up a storm with the first letter, wanting to be back, and it was easy, in the face of all that damage, to simply avoid it from then on by removing the cause, the letters.

Oh, the lies we tell ourselves.

We darn them as we would a hole in a sock until they are robust and thorough, until they have mended the hole. And we take it off the darning egg and we hold it up to the light. And if we can't see the play of damage and darn, we call it a job well done.

Years of letters fed to the fire. My poor mother, abandoned all the same, she thought, by whom she held most dear. My poor Ellen, abandoned in New York, while her daughter lived a life she might have had, in other times. And poor Annie, in the middle of it, trying to smooth over what can't be smoothed over, what sticks to the inside of a life and burrs whenever we breathe.

HERE, IN THE PRIVACY OF THIS PAGE, by my hand, are those letters now. I wish I could show you: that nothing more than a wooden desk separates us, and nothing more than this darning hand might somehow set to rights.

Have it anyway, for what it's worth. A paragraph in a letter, perhaps. One small but truthful episode in a tale darned with small lies.

Here is the fire. Here is the woman bent over it, feeding two sets of pages to the flames. And here is the smoke from that fire, whitened with paper and blackened by words, rising up from a Ballyhaunis chimney, blown west over the town roofs and west over the fields and the ditches beyond, blown all the way to the Mayo coast, out over the ocean, where it drifts and drifts and dissipates in the sky above water, so every trace of it and all it means and all it knew and the hurt in the words and the hurt that wasn't—simply disappear.

WORDS: I DON'T KNOW ANY OTHER WAY TO TELL THE STORY. Here I am scratching them out of thin air, slipping some of them over to you by a sleight of hand that fools no one, I know that.

I am in your city, here for nine months, on my own, with your life in my hands. Before me, it was my mother's city for the first twelve years of her life. Before that, it was her mother's city, that she came back to aged thirteen and lived in until she was thirty-seven, with a husband and four children and a mother who'd made a life for herself between servants' attics and boarders' lodgings; between putting by and getting by; between letters, between plans.

Before that, it was yours.

I came with money in my pocket, a fellowship, and an address. Hardly a risk; more an adventure, and I wanted it badly, to live awhile in the stories my mother would tell me, hour on hour, cigarette on cigarette, until my father would come in the kitchen and ask, "Would you not let this child go to bed and tomorrow a school day?"

She was lonely, I suppose, and the stories were company. Seeing *King Kong* that time with her father in Radio City Music Hall. The Wall Street crash. Rudolph Valentino's funeral, her mother crying for hours in the bathroom in her Sunday best. The boardwalk at Rockaway Beach, someone taking the pram with her little brother in it, and her running around like a mad yoke, peering into every pram until she found his bright blue eyes. Sledding in Riverside Park, the speed of it running away with her and her fright in her throat, until it just stopped in a bank of snow and she was tossed, unhurt except for the new knowledge of fear and what it can do to you.

A photograph of her, dumpty and squinting, in Central Park when she was three.

A photograph of her Confirmation Day, aged eleven, when she didn't know that all she knew was about to turn to water under her.

A photograph taken on the deck of the *Scythia*, when she was sailing back.

Her granny, abandoned. No photograph, no letter, no memento, no solid proof.

My mother built a Manhattan of stories in a Co. Westmeath kitchen, and I loved the sound of it.

Of course it was where I wanted to be, then and since, for who can resist a city of stories, a city built behind the city, that exists only for you?

I say I came here on my own, but that's not strictly true. I came with a notional suitcase packed edge to edge with bits and bobs of borrowed memories. When I got to the New York Public Library in Bryant Park, I had it with me in my office, and I unpacked it, slip by slip, until they filled the room to the ceiling, from the window to the door.

Some days, I would pull on a thread and hear my mother's voice.

Some days, my grandmother's, reedy because I didn't know her well and only when she was old.

And some days, yours.

Nine months of listening and looking; nine months of poking in "evidence," and nine months of listening between words for what I could convince myself could be what I was looking for.

THE CEMETERY OFFICE GIVES ME a set of numbers I try to graft onto the cemetery map. Section 21, plot 83, Calvary Third in Queens (where people from Manhattan go to die).

An Ellen O'Grady is buried there. It may even be you.

And it is. Unless another woman with your name had another son with the same name, born in the year Jimmy was born, it is you. It has to be.

I'm delighted to see no year of birth is given: I'll warrant you would not have stood for so bald and artless a truth, while maybe also preferring not to be buried under a flat lie.

So there we have it: a bookend, a closed bracket, one last fact. I know when you died and where your bones are laid. Right beside the Queens Expressway, tucked under in a plot on which the sun can't shine because the road blocks out all the light. But there's a little scrub of bush, and you could think of the traffic noise as a lullaby, if you so desired.

The headstone is limestone, smaller than the one behind it, with pretty flowers carved in the two top corners and, under the names, the best possible end to a life of shuffling continents and families and work; of plaiting together here and there, of managing things as best you could in a life that went against plan. Two words (after all these words), and a simple claim.

At Rest.

I tell you all about my life, and while I'm there, my daughter calls the cell phone and I show her your headstone and I rest my hand there until either it cools in the stone-cold minutes, or the stone warms, fractionally, to my skin.

And then I take the No. 7 train back to my desk, where I put down these words.

"Today, in her lap, is a wooden-handle magnifying glass;
   she expects, looks like, to have to undertake a search.
   She wears a red cloche with a brooch of bird feathers
   she sees me admiring. "No, you can't have it," she says.
   Then smiles. "I left what I had to Jimmy. It wasn't much.
   My lucky wedding ring, a good enough wristwatch.
   Gewgaws from the boarding house: vases, rugs, and such.
   Old clothes. Those few long ago letters from my father.

"God knows where it is now, that stuff. He gave each
   of my sisters something, I suppose. A small keepsake.
   Posted Annie a box in Ireland, maybe: bits and pieces
   including, for Helen, the Japanese tea set she used to like
   that I promised (and forgot) to send to Ireland after her.
   If it survived the voyage, I doubt it survived the years."

SURVIVE, IT DID. I KNOW THAT TEA SET. A russet band around the rim, and a Japanese scene on both sides with flowers in deep blue. I have it now, or what's left of it, a couple of wide-brimmed, imperfect cups ideal, I'd say, for tea-leaf readings, were I so inclined.

Ellen would have gone to America with a single bag of all she owned in the world. My mother, Helen, will have come back from there with a trunk, no doubt, of what it had been decided she could not do without. I have moved to America in the past, with furniture and toys and art in frames, and I moved the selfsame furniture and all back again when we didn't want to stay. It's just stuff. We shimmy it around the world as though it were somehow abstracted, incorporeal, despite the weight of it in our hands or the money we fork out to have it shipped. We are surprised when the moving van shows up and all of it, far too much of it, is disgorged upon clean, new lives. We struggle with finding a place for it all. We swear we will discard half and of course, we never do.

But what wouldn't I give for those letters? Even for a single one of them.

The teacups are in another country now, but I have them in my mind. They could break, every single one of them; I'd still have them in mind.

Which means I can still hold them to the window here, three thousand miles from where they are, to notice once again the depth of blue.

You're not listening. You're playing with your magnifying glass, tilting it so it catches the light from the standing lamp beside you and bounces it up onto the wall on the other side of the room. You are tending that little glob of light as if you were a lighthouse keeper, and it is all that stands between every passing ship and harm.

That light, reflected by your hand, is the light by which I imagine I see the cells in the bloodline that connects us, three generations down.

"So you know it now from start to end: caboodle, kit, the lot,
ins and outs, back and forth, the what, when, why, why not.
You started with my name and, fact by fact, you reeled me in
until here I am, have been for years, in a family plot in Queens.
If it *is* me." You smile. Your hand at your lips is a question mark,
but no question between us was not resolved in the half-dark
under the Queens Expressway, when I yabbered at your grave
about my book, your Ellie (my Helen), my children, all our lives.

And kneeling to take a photo of your headstoned name
I saw it gleaming in brown earth where grass should be,
the clear glass pebble with the only light in it I took away
and keep by me: the stone made of glass I choose to see
as gift as much as my slantwise words, your hereafter story,
as gift as much as the blood, lifeline, in my children's veins.

ELLEN: MY GHOST.

Or, in the sense that I'm a remnant of you, an aftermath, I suppose I must be yours.

Ellen, my ghostwriter.

Who takes her ease in complicit silence as streets do when they cross each other; as lives do, on the page.

Who bristles as streetlamps coming on; who clears her throat as if clogged with words; who hums as lightbulbs do when they are giving up the ghost.

Who remembers as a door will do who passes in and out.

Who counts her hereafter as blanket stitches along an infinite hem.

Who looks in shop windows for the face puddled in the yard at home. Who is sorry, fleetingly, to be answered by the nothing there.

Who buttons her absence against every forecast I care to throw at her.

Who writes, if she writes, with an innocent pen on a page that isn't there. Who angers when I can't read it to her. Who asks if I am blind.

Who carries a name like a stone in her pocket. Who counts on the weight of it.

Who thinks I remind her of someone, but can't say as to whom.

Who would have me believe she cannot be here.

Who smirks the way shadow does, in snatches, if I choose to do.

Whose watching is done with mirrors on a wheel I may have spun, or she did, or I do, so our watching is like water slipping into water, or shadow falling upon shadow, or a fact singled out from a lifetime of facts and made big, so it hides all the others.

IN CALVARY, I TOLD YOU THAT BOTH your children lived long lives. That Annie, my grandmother, died in Mayo in 1984. That you have a living granddaughter, my aunt Mary, and more great-grandchildren than I know, living in Ireland and the United States, and probably other places too.

That those great-grandchildren also have grandchildren.

That my daughter's middle name is Ellen.

That she will have the watch.

It is snowing as i type, Fifth Avenue outside my office window gray as if every cell of daylight has a small lead weight inside. You must have known many such an evening, in all your New York years. Gray like the stone walls of Glenavoo. Gray like the swell of an ocean when the wind is getting up. Gray the way being lonely is gray, your family far away from you and nothing to do with the raw love you feel except to put the words of it down and hope they will come to a soft landing and have more purchase there than weather on wet pavements and the year's remaining leaves.

I am writing words as if they were tilted up to falling snow so these particular words are lost in a flurry of all possible words that could tell a simple truth.

I am sorry that your life was hard, grateful you did what you could. I hope you never wished the money you sent home back to you; that someone, at least, said thank you to you and your sisters for your many sacrifices (for they were surely that) so that you could protect your parents from a callous and niggardly wind.

And I hope you were not forgotten when the farm was secure, the animals fed, and the house robust. That the dimming of a Sligo fire rhymed with the light you switched on against such an evening as this. That your accent rhymed with your children's, the same meld of New York and Sligo that set you apart from (almost) everyone, and made a home of you three. That the money in the family account rhymed very nicely with the money you managed to save in your own.

That your children cherished you, and your grandchildren (I know my mother did).

That mistakes made or liberties taken in the telling of this are no offence to your memory, which I mean only to honor even after so many years.

It is almost dark. The lights of the city crowd into my office. From my second-floor window, everybody looks urgent and dark. Of course you would have passed by here, you might even have come inside betimes to climb, as I do, these marble steps and to sit under ambitious, painted clouds to imagine a summer's day.

You might have looked up to this very window. And, seeing nothing and no one there, have gone on home.

END

"Fifth Avenue, Snow." View from author's office window: room 14, Cullman Center, New York Public Library.

Acknowledgments

This book arose out of a chance encounter with Ellen one lunch-break archive search during my fellowship at the Cullman Center at the New York Public Library. My thanks go to my fellow Fellows there for their nicely shared and impossibly huge knowledge-base, and to Salvatore Scibona, Lauren Goldenberg, and Paul Delaverda for their many and generous steers.

This was once a baggier book: several people read it in its various incarnations and helped me to distinguish between the interestingly specific and irredeemably arcane. To Conor O'Callaghan, Tommy O'Callaghan, Eve O'Callaghan (who also knew just when to phone), Frances Wilson, Paul Keegan, Maree Lundon, Ray Groarke, Ray Ryan and Colette Bryce, I owe a debt of thanks I'll probably never repay (because, honestly, who could?).

To Clara Platter, New York University Press, and the Glucks-man Irish Diaspora Series, my thanks and sincere admiration for the creative editing that made room for Ellen, giving her a new home in New York.

To my colleagues at the Centre for New Writing in the University of Manchester for their support while writing this.

Lastly, to Ellen and to all the Ellens who worked so hard and made such a difference, in the United States and at home.

Because they really ought to be thanked, even after so many years.

Bibliography

Anbinder, Tyler. "Moving beyond Rags to Riches: New York's Irish Famine Immigrants and Their Surprising Savings Accounts." *Journal of American History* 99, no. 3 (December 2012): 741–70.

An Gorta Mór: Famine in the Swinford Union. Swinford: Swinford Historical Society, 1995.

Barrett, James R. *The Irish Way: Becoming American in the Multiethnic City.* New York: Penguin, 2012.

Bayer, Ronald H., and Timothy J Meagher, eds. *The New York Irish.* Baltimore, MD: John Hopkins University Press, 1996.

Bloom, Ester. "The Decline of Domestic Help." *Atlantic*, September 23, 2015. *www.theatlantic.com.*

Byron, Joseph. *Photographs of New York Interiors at the Turn of the Century.* New York: Dover, 1976.

Casey, Marion R. "Emigrant as Historian: Records, Banking, and Irish-American Scholarship." *American Journal of Irish Studies* 10 (2013): 145–63.

Cohen, Deborah. *Family Secrets: Living with Shame from the Victorians to the Present Day.* London: Viking, 2013.

Colum, Padraic. *The Road around Ireland.* New York: Macmillan, 1926.

Connolly, James. *The Re-Conquest of Ireland.* Dublin: New Books, [1915] 1968.

Crowley, John, William J. Smyth, and Mike Murphy. *Atlas of the Great Irish Famine.* New York: New York University Press, 2012.

Diner, Hasia R. *Erin's Daughters in America: Irish Immigrant Women in the Nineteenth Century.* Baltimore, MD: Johns Hopkins University Press, 1983.

———. "The Accidental Irish." In *Migration in History*, edited by Marc S. Rodriguez and Anthony T. Grafton, 118–60. Rochester, NY: University of Rochester Press, 2007.

Doan, Robert A. "Green Gold to the Emerald Shores: Irish Immigration to the United States and Transatlantic Monetary Aid, 1854–1923." PhD diss., Temple University, 1999.

Dooley, Terence. *The Big Houses and Landed Estates of Ireland.* Dublin: Four Courts, 2007.

Dudden, Faye E. *Serving Women: Household Service in Nineteenth-Century America.* Middletown, CT: Wesleyan University Press, 1983.

Dufferin and Ava, Marquess of. *Irish Emigration and the Tenure of Land in Ireland.* London: Willis, Southeran, 1867.

Elias, Megan J. *Food in the United States, 1890–1945.* Santa Barbara, CA: Greenwood, 2009.

Ewen, Elizabeth. *Immigrant Women in the Land of Dollars*. New York: Monthly Review, 1985.

Ferris, Tom. *The Trains Long Departed: Ireland's Lost Railways*. Dublin: Gill & Macmillan, 2010.

Fitzpatrick, David. *Irish Emigration, 1801–1921*. Dundalk: Dun Dealgan, 1984.

Flynn, Peter. "How Bridget Was Framed: The Irish Domestic in Early American Cinema, 1895–1917." *Cinema Journal* 50, no. 2 (Winter 2011): 1–20.

Fortner, Robert S. "The Culture of Hope and the Culture of Despair: The Print Media and Nineteenth-Century Emigration." *Eire-Ireland* 13, no. 3 (Autumn 1978): 32–48.

Gamber, Wendy. *The Boarding House in Nineteenth-Century America*. Baltimore, MD: John Hopkins University Press, 2007.

Guinnane, Timothy. *The Vanishing Irish: Households, Migration, and the Rural Economy of Ireland, 1850–1914*. Princeton, NJ: Princeton University Press, 1997.

Gunn, Thomas Butler. *The Physiology of New York Boarding Houses*. Edited by David Faflik. New Brunswick, NJ: Rutgers University Press, 2009. First published 1857 by Mason Brothers (New York).

Hamrock, Ivor, ed. *The Famine in Mayo, 1845–1850*. Castlebar, Mayo County Council, 2004.

Harris, Ruth-Ann. "'Come All You Courageously': Irish Women in America Write Home." *Éire-Ireland* 36, nos. 1–2 (Spring–Summer 2001): 166–84.

Hooker, Elizabeth. *Readjustments of Agricultural Tenure in Ireland*. Chapel Hill: University of North Carolina Press, 1938.

Hotten-Somers, Diane. "Relinquishing and Reclaiming Independence: Irish Domestic Servants, American Middle-Class Mistresses, and Assimilation, 1850–1920." In *New Directions in Irish-American History*, edited by Kevin Kenny, 227-242. Madison: University of Wisconsin Press, 2003.

Jackson, Pauline. "Women in Nineteenth-Century Irish Emigration." *International Migration Review* 18, no. 4 (Winter 1984): 1004–20.

Kennedy, Liam, Paul Ell, E. M. Crawford, and L. A. Clarkson. *Mapping the Great Irish Famine: A Survey of the Famine Decades*. Dublin: Four Courts, 1999.

Kennedy, Robert Emmet. *The Irish: Emigration, Marriage and Fertility*. Berkeley: University of California Press, 1973.

Kenny, Kevin. *The American Irish*. Harlow: Pearson Education, 2000.

———. "Irish Emigration, c. 1845–1900." In *The Cambridge History of Ireland*, vol. 2, ed. James Kelly, 666–87. Cambridge: Cambridge University Press, 2018.

Killen, John. ed. *The Famine Decades: Contemporary Accounts, 1841–1851*. Belfast: Blackstaff, 1995.

Kinealy, Christine. *This Great Calamity: The Irish Famine, 1845–52*. New York: Roberts Rinehart, 1995.

———. *The Great Irish Famine: Impact, Ideology, and Rebellion*. Hampshire: Palgrave Macmillan, 2002.

Kissane, Noel. *The Irish Famine: A Documentary History*. Dublin: National Library of Ireland, 1995.

Lee, Joseph. *The Modernisation of Irish Society, 1848–1918*. Dublin: Gill & Macmillan, 1973.

Lobel, Cindy R. *Urban Appetites: Food and Culture in Nineteenth-Century New York*. Chicago: University of Chicago Press, 2014.

Lynch-Brennan, Margaret. "Ubiquitous Bridget: Irish Immigrant Women in Domestic Service in America, 1840–1930." In *Making the Irish American*, edited by J. J. Lee and Marion R. Casey, 332–53. New York: New York University Press, 2006.

———. *The Irish Bridget: Irish Immigrant Women in Domestic Service in America, 1840–1930*. Syracuse, NY: Syracuse University Press, 2009.

MacSuibhne, Breandán. *The End of Outrage: Post-Famine Adjustment in Rural Ireland*. Oxford: Oxford University Press, 2017.

McDonnell, Colleen. "Going to the Ladies Fair: Irish Catholics in New York City, 1870–1900." In *The New York Irish*, edited by Ronald Bayer and Timothy Meagher, 234–51. Baltimore, MD: John Hopkins University Press, 1996.

McTernan, John C., *Sligo: The Light of Bygone Days; Sligo Families: Chronicles of Sixty Families Past and Present*. Sligo: Aveena, 2009.

Magee, Gary, and Andrew Thompson. "Lines of Credit, Debts of Obligation: Migrant Remittances to Britain c. 1875–1913." *Economic History Review* 59, no. 3 (August 2006): 539–77.

Maguire, John Francis. *The Irish in America*. New York: Arno, [1868] 1969.

Maynard Salman, Lucy. *Domestic Service*. New York: Macmillan, 1911.

Meaney, Geraldine, Mary O'Dowd, and Bernadette Whelan. *Reading the Irish Woman: Studies in Cultural Encounters and Exchange, 1714–1960*. Liverpool: Liverpool University Press, 2013.

Miller, Kerby. *Emigrants and Exiles: Ireland and the Irish Exodus to North America*. Oxford: Oxford University Press, 1985.

———. *Ireland and Irish America: Culture, Class, and Transatlantic Migration*. Dublin: Field Day, 2008.

Mokyr, Joel. *Why Ireland Starved: A Quantitative and Analytical History of the Irish Economy, 1800–1850*. London: Allen & Unwin, 1983.

Murphy, Maureen. "The Fionnuala Factor: Irish Sibling Emigration at the Turn of the Century." In *Gender and Sexuality in Modern Ireland*, edited by Anthony Bradley and Maryann Gialanella Valiulis, 85–101. Amherst: University of Massachusetts Press, 1997.

———. "The Irish Servant Girl in Literature." *Writing Ulster*, 5 (1998): 133–47.

———. "Bridget and Biddy: Images of the Irish Servant Girl in Puck Cartoons, 1880–1890." In *New Perspectives on the Irish Diaspora*, edited by Charles Fanning, 152–75. Carbondale: Southern Illinois University Press, 2000.

Nicholson, Asenath. *Annals of the Famine in Ireland*. Edited by Maureen Murphy. Dublin: Lilliput, 1998.

Nolan, Janet A. *Ourselves Alone: Women's Emigration from Ireland, 1885–1920*. Lexington: University Press of Kentucky, 1989.

Ó Gráda, Cormac. *Ireland: A New Economic History*. Oxford: Oxford University Press, 1984.

———. *Ireland before and after the Famine: Explorations in Economic History, 1800–1925*. 2nd ed. Manchester: Manchester University Press, 1993.

———. *The Great Irish Famine*. Cambridge: Cambridge University Press, 1996.

———. *Ireland's Great Famine: Interdisciplinary Perspectives*. Dublin: University College Dublin, 2006.

Paul-Dubois, Louis. *Contemporary Ireland*. Dublin: Baker & Taylor, 1908.

Pomfret, John E. *The Struggle for Land in Ireland*. Princeton, NJ: Princeton University Press, 1930.

Ray, Celeste. "Paying the Rounds at Ireland's Holy Wells." *Anthropos* 110, no. 2 (2015): 415–32.

Rhodes, Rita M., *Women and the Family in Post-Famine Ireland*. New York: Garland, 1992.

Schrier, Arnold. *Ireland and Irish Emigration to the New World*. Minneapolis: University of Minnesota Press, 1958.

Shrout, Anelise H. "The Famine and New York City." In *Atlas of the Great Irish Famine*, edited by John Crowley, William J. Smyth and Mike Murphy, 536–46. New York: New York University Press, 2012.

Smyth, William J. "Exodus from Ireland—Patterns of Emigration." In *Atlas of the Great Irish Famine*, edited by John Crowley, William J. Smyth and Mike Murphy, 494–503. New York: New York University Press, 2012.

Solow, Barbara. *The Land Question and the Irish Economy, 1870–1903*. Cambridge, MA: Harvard University Press, 1971.

Strasser, Susan. *Never Done: A History of American Housework*. New York: Pantheon, 1982.

Sutherland, Daniel E. *Americans and Their Servants: Domestic Service in the United States from 1800 to 1920*. Baton Rouge: Louisiana State University Press, 1981.

Swords, Liam. *In Their Own Words: The Famine in North Connacht, 1845–1849*. Dublin: Columba, 1999.

Tóibín, Colm, and Diarmaid Ferriter. *The Irish Famine: A Documentary*. London: Profile, 2001.

Tuke, James Hack. *A Visit to Connaught in the Autumn of 1847; a Letter Addressed to the Central Relief Committee of the Society of Friends*. London: Gilpin, 1848.

Urban, Andrew. "Irish Domestic Servants, 'Biddy,' and Rebellion in the American Home, 1850–1900." *Gender and History* 21, no. 2 (August 2009): 263–86.

Vaughan, W. E. *Landlords and Tenants in Mid-Victorian Ireland*. Oxford: Clarendon, 1994.

Wittke, Carl. *The Irish in America*. Baton Rouge: Louisiana State University Press, 1956.

About the Author

One of Ireland's leading poets, **VONA GROARKE** has published eight poetry collections, most recently *Link: Poet and World* (The Gallery Press, 2021). Her *Selected Poems* was winner of the 2017 Pigott Prize for Best Irish Poetry Collection. A Cullman Fellow at the New York Public Library (2018–19), she has taught creative writing at the University of Manchester since 2007 and is the current Poet in Residence at St John's College, University of Cambridge. Essayist, editor, reviewer, and critic, she is a member of Aosdána (the Irish Academy of Artists). She makes her home in rural Sligo in the west of Ireland, where she reads and writes.

**GLUCKSMAN
IRISH DIASPORA**

IN THE GLUCKSMAN IRISH DIASPORA SERIES
EDITED BY KEVIN KENNY